TALES FROM THE DEEP

To Ed,

Fellow shipmate and
great friend,

Jo Kun

IN THE BEGINNING...

"Are we there yet? Are we there yet?"

How many times, while traveling, have we heard the grandkids say these four words over and over again? And, of course, there's only one answer:

"No, we're still here."

"Where?"

"Right here."

"Where's here?"

"On the road to there."

"Oh."

As I write these words, we're still not there. There, of course, is another reunion of those who served aboard the USS *Manatee*. But we might as well be there because I already have the vision— old codgers all, in their mid-50s to the 90s the oldest. I'm among them watching as the other old guys come in the door.

None of us have the snappy white uniforms of summer or the dark blue of winter. And the perfectly formed white hats have now been replaced by the equally white hair or no hair at all. The spry step is now a much slower stride. But the mind, the will and the memories are there. And boy, do we have the memories!

It's those memories that make up the better part of this book. They were compiled through cooperation of these former *Manatee* Sailors, officers and enlisted men alike, who came through when asked. At the same time, however, it should be noted that there were a lot of our former shipmates who once served aboard the ship that couldn't be located. And of those that were tracked down, many, because of failing health or other reasons, were not able to contribute.

Now, all legends are built upon facts—and there are a lot of them included in this book. But because some of us have on occasion been a little fuzzy with the dates or particulars, don't hold our feet to the fire on this. And although we did our best to tell it like it was, none who participated here raised their hands in sworn testimony before offering their thoughts.

Remember this: When we served we were all very young—19 to 25-year-olds for the most part. Most of us were far away from our homes for the first time. As a result we didn't think we were that responsible for our actions. If we went astray for a time we were thinking we would chalk it up to poor judgment. We certainly wouldn't dream of repeating any of the off-duty and sometimes on-duty misdeeds today. Absolutely! That's for certain! No way!

Now, for you former *Manatee* Sailors: If any of you feel complimented by what others tell about you here—that's good. However, if a story or two mentions your name and it happens to be just a little bit embarrassing, then remember what shipmate Ray Hooper told us: Sailors have a tendency on occasion to exaggerate.

So, if it's something you would just as soon forget—you are not required to believe a word of it. After all, all of this was a long time ago. Your denials may just be enough to get you off the hook with a wife or significant other. And for the rest of us—we are a forgiving lot.

So, here we are—at where it all begins: The situation of reporting aboard the ship for the first time. For me, as a 20-year-old, I stood, orders in hand, (as many others did), at the end of the gangplank. I looked up (again, as others did), to the ship beside the pier. There was no preparation for the site before our eyes.

I guess all of us were expecting for our first Navy assignment, a sleek-looking cruiser or an aircraft carrier with a fancy name like the *Enterprise* or the *Hornet* with all those great-looking airplanes about. Instead, this ship was not sleek nor was it necessarily good looking. Well, let's face it—the *Manatee* was a floating gas station. What would I tell my friends back home?

But looks were deceiving. For what a ship she was! And what an adventure!

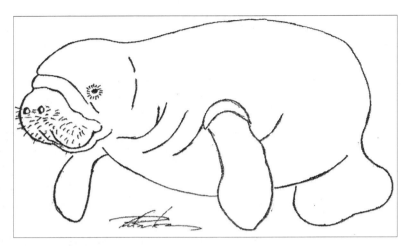

The USS *Manatee* was named after the *Manatee* River in Florida, not the river mammal as many believed. The river, however, was named after the mammal which inhabited its waters. Go figure!

CHAPTER 1

1944-1945 THE BIRTH OF A LEGEND
INTO THE HEAT OF BATTLE

During World War II comedian Milton Berle was asked to christen a supply ship at the Brooklyn Navy Yard. For him this was serious and he wasn't about to do any funny business. So, with the champagne bottle held in place with a rope, he tossed the bottle toward the bow. It missed. So again he tossed the bottle toward the target and again it missed. A third time would be a charm—well, maybe. At this point one of the officers shook his head and said, "Maybe you could hold the bottle still, and we'll aim the ship at it!

There was no such incident when the USS *Manatee* (AO-58) was christened and launched February 18, 1944. In fact, all went along as planned as the Cimarron-class fleet replenishment oiler drifted out into the Chesapeake Bay from the Bethlehem Sparrows Point Shipyard in Maryland. What followed was a 10-day shakedown period in the Bay before the *Manatee* headed out for the Dutch West Indies, where it loaded up its tanks with oil.

The *Manatee* was a long, broad-beamed oiler of unusual speed and maneuverability, designed expressly for fueling ships at sea. Her power plant was built around four steam turbines which, coupled with the usual oiler propulsion of twin screws, gave the ship the speed necessary to operate with the ships of the Navy at that time. She was armed with moderate sized guns and in her tanks were 120,000 barrels of oil and aviation gasoline.

The details: Laid down: August 28, 1943. Launched: Feb. 18, 1944. Commissioned: April 6, 1944. Displacement: 7,236 tons (light), 25,440 tons (full). Length: 533 feet. Beam: 75 feet. Draft: 32 feet, four inches. Propulsion: geared turbines, twin screws. Speed: 18 knots. Complement: 314 officers and enlisted. Armament: one single 5"/38 gun mounts, four single 3"/50 dual purpose gun mounts, four twin 40mm gun mounts and four twin 20mm gun mounts.

The Sailors, new to the Navy and who were aboard a ship for the first time, however, were probably not paying much attention to the *Manatee*'s details. Their concern was first, where could they find some food? And second, where was the bathroom? The food, of course, had a new name. Here it was the appropriately named—the mess. And for that second necessity, it had a new name as well—the head. In those old sailing ship days this convenience was always located at the front of the ship: the head, in other words. No longer, now those bathrooms, or heads as they are called, are located near all the sleeping quarters. That could be anywhere. But rather than going to the trouble of changing the name, the Navy just kept it.

All of this, of course, was the beginnings of a new vocabulary that wasn't taught in those language arts classes at school. In the Navy, the bridge, for instance, wasn't a place to cross over in your trip to the park or from which you could dangle a fishing pole.

Here the bridge is the raised platform toward the front of the ship. Here is the steering and the headquarters of all that is important. A bulkhead was not a person with a big head, but the vertical partitions (or walls) separating each part of the ship. The two-word term 'man overboard', meant just that. And that, of course, was to be avoided at all costs. Affecting them most, however, was the term, "work party." Sailors soon learned that it was not the after-hours fun gatherings like it sounded. Work: yes. Party: no.

*   *   *

On launch day it was Lieutenant Commander Joseph B. Smith who was assigned as the skipper of the *Manatee*. He would serve until December 23, 1945. His first orders were to take the *Manatee* through the Panama Canal. That experience, of course, is prime for present-day vacations on those air conditioned cruise ships, complete with elevators between decks, swimming pools and nightcaps awaiting you at the bar. None of these amenities, of course, existed on the *Manatee*. What the Sailors did have were all those personal cameras. On that Atlantic Ocean to Pacific Ocean trip through the Panama Canal it was time to put them to use.

The first order, after maneuvering the ship through the canal, was now ready to be undertaken. And that was for the ship to head for the war zone in the Pacific as quickly as possible. Here, of course, is where people would be shooting at you and you were expected to shoot back.

For the *Manatee*, however, shooting back wasn't the prime mission. What was, was the job of keeping other ships in fuel so they could take on this wartime responsibility. What wasn't mentioned was something one gradually realized on his own.

And that was the fact that oilers, like the *Manatee*, were prime targets for the enemy. Wipe out an oiler and you can also put many other warships in jeopardy.

The Navy Brass, of course, knew this and devised a plan during wartime to make such an attack unlikely at best. To do this, ships

That first day of refueling was a difficult one, starting at 9 a.m. and ending at 7:05 p.m. This 10 hours of non-stop operations resulted in damage to a fueling rig when the *Manatee* suffered a steering casualty. But by the time the ship went into action a few days later, it was well prepared when the battleship *USS Indiana* came alongside. It was fueled and departed all in a minimum of time and without difficulty.

Before a refueling operation takes place, the captain takes personal command of the ship. Phone communication is established from the bridge to the receiving ship or ships. At the helm is the most experienced helmsman on the ship. And, should something unforeseen happen in this area, another helmsman is stationed in the emergency manual steering compartment located in the rear of the ship.

Prior to the war, mid-ocean refueling was rare and even more dangerous than it was when the *Manatee* was on duty in the Pacific. In the early years only one ship could be replenished at a time. And there was only one hose, which stretched from the fantail (back of the ship) to the bow (up front). Recent major advancements enabled two ships to be replenished at one time, one on each side of an oiler. When situations demand it, even a third vessel could be refueled astern. Now with having multiple hoses they all could be operating at the same time and be going in different directions. Some would be used for transferring just ship's oil, others aviation gas for aircraft carrier airplanes.

Praising the oiler crews, Admiral Chester Nimitz, who commanded the Pacific Fleet at the time, said, "not many an oiler will ever be able to paint a Japanese battle flag, for planes downed or ships sunk, upon her bridge, but every man in the task force is aware of the importance of the contribution of these service ships."

Admiral Nimitz

Even though most of the islands were still occupied by the Japanese when the *Manatee* arrived for duty, the object was to reverse the situation. If captured, these islands were considered prime spots for the construction of airfields from which the new B-29 bombers could attack Japan itself. So one by one, American and allied forces attacked and eventually succeeded in their efforts, but only after heavy costs of lives on both sides.

In the case of Guam, it fell on August 9th to U.S. forces after 20 days of bloody fighting. The conquest cost the Americans 1,214 dead and nearly 6,000 wounded. A total of 17,000 Japanese were killed, many of these by suicide. Some 500 Japanese simply gave up and were taken prisoner. However, there were a number of Japanese that rejected both suicide and capture. So they hid in the jungle and reappeared after the war was over, in one case 27 years after the Japanese surrender.

*   *   *

General MacArthur

General Douglas MacArthur disobeyed orders to defend the Philippines in what was known to be a certain attack. In the process, not only were many lives lost, but virtually his entire air force and other vital assets were eliminated. It left the island country virtually defenseless as the Japanese invaders landed on its beaches.

Because it was now wartime, President Roosevelt had no choice but to keep him in place in what would in normal times necessitate an automatic court-martial. And to further cover-up MacArthur's debacle, the President gave MacArthur the nation's highest honor, a Medal of Honor. Then, in March of 1942, the President ordered him out of harm's way to regroup in Australia. The plan was to invade the Philippines in full force, supported by the U.S. Navy's Third Fleet with every gun and plane it could muster. The *Manatee* was a vital part of this plan as all of these vessels would be needing fuel. On August 20, the *Manatee* moved to Manus, largest of the Admiralty Islands. Here the ship continued carrying fuel and other supplies to fast carrier groups through the Battle for Pele Lieu and other campaigns. By October 20, when the *Manatee* departed Manus for the last time, Ulithi Atoll had been secured and had become the center for oilers.

*   *   *

The *Manatee* was front and center supporting the forces then covering the Luzon landings in the Philippines. In the operation, a task force of 850 ships sailed into Lingayen Gulf, 100 miles North of Manila. The battle, which transpired from October 23-26, 1944, was to be the last classical naval battle and the largest naval battle in history, with opposing surface ships actually in sight of each other.

At the time the Japanese had few naval aircraft left, and even fewer experienced crews. But what they had was a well-thought-out plan and they made good use of their strength in battleships and cruisers. Yet, while they took out two U.S. carriers, the *Gambier Bay* and the *Princeton*, Japan lost two heavy cruisers, three carriers and three battleships-the *Fuso*, the *Yamashiro* and the *Musashi*. The Japanese, who at one
time had been close to a victory in this battle, had in the end sustained a crushing defeat.

The fleet at that time was commanded by the rawboned seaman of slender build, Admiral William "Bull" Halsey. An early riser, he was known to drink 10 cups of coffee and smoke 40 cigarettes in a day. In the evening he would top this off with a glass of Scotch whiskey-alcohol that was forbidden for the general crew. Idiosyncrasies aside, he was known as the best of what the U.S. Navy had to offer and was highly respected by those who served under him.

Admiral Halsey

17

But now he was faced by his most difficult set of circumstances. And the decision he made still haunts military historians to this day. His decision was between (1) to help MacArthur in his amphibious landings on the island of Mindoro in the Philippines, as was his orders, or (2) to disobey these orders to get the fleet out of harm's way of what was to be a major typhoon. His decision was to help MacArthur and stay to ride out the storm.

Named Typhoon Cobra, the storm turned out to be one of the worst ever experienced by the U.S. Navy. As is typical in the Luzon Strait, this typhoon covered an area of about 300 miles in diameter with the cloud bands extending up to 65 miles in circumference. Here, typhoons tend to be the fiercest on the planet with winds up to 250 knots. Had the fleet tried to outrun the storm, it's not clear, even in hindsight, if this would have succeeded.

Three *Manatee* Sailors, George W. Smith, Royce Godwin and Eugene "Red" Seeley were among those aboard the *Manatee* at that time and later recalled when it met its most major test of endurance. It all started on December 17, when word came of the approaching typhoon. The storm was heading directly in the path of the *Manatee* and several other ships waiting to be refueled at sea. So, quickly, in heavy seas and while the weather conditions were growing steadily worse, the destroyers *Lyman K. Swenson* (DD-729) and *Maddox* (DD-731) were refueled as was the aircraft carrier *Hancock* (CV-19).

"I ran the steam winch," Seeley said. "And on that day I was positioned on the cargo deck above the well deck. My job was to keep the hoses above water. It wasn't easy. Water rushed between the vessels which got as close as nine feet."

But it wasn't before the destroyers suffered heavy damage to their fueling rigs and lost several sections of hose and tending lines when the ships were driven apart by the heavy seas.

"That night Royce and I were sleeping on the well deck," Smith said. "But it wasn't for long. In the middle of the night the storm worsened and we were abruptly awakened when water came over the side. Each of the waves went totally over us, soaking us completely. Somehow we managed to get up, hold on and get back to our compartment. And somehow we managed to get some sleep despite the rough seas."

Smith said that if that wasn't bad enough, things worsened the next morning. "When trying to eat breakfast, food and trays alike were flying about like we've never experienced before. Eating was impossible."

Seeley remembered well those days, "When the winds hit the top of the waves, the spray of the water was like needles hitting you in the face."

As the storm reached its peak, the two most used words by everyone aboard were "hold on!" The ship drove through the heavy seas at slow speed, taking the huge waves over her bow and decks while smothered in fine salt spray that all but hit the after part of the ship from the bridge. Movement from one enclosed part of the ship to another became impossible due to unbroken succession of waves being swept over the connecting catwalks.

"We had to stay low in the water so we wouldn't break in half," Seeley said. "We took on sea water into empty fuel tanks and even put water on top of the oil in tanks that were only partially filled. This would keep us from bouncing around so much."

Smith said that while the *Manatee* survived the storm without any major damage to the ship and without any injuries to its crew, the other ships didn't fare as well. "It was unbelievable to see the damage the typhoon did to them," he said. "It's something I hope I never have to see again."

Seeley said that during the worst of it, waves tossed the ships around like toys as the powerful storm's winds flexed at 116 miles per hour. He said that three destroyers capsized and quickly sank, taking most aboard to the bottom of the sea. It was reported later that a total of 793 men were lost and 80 more were injured. In addition to the three ships that were lost, another dozen ships had been rendered inoperable and 146 aircraft, attached to aircraft carriers, were lost or damaged beyond repair. The Third Fleet was decimated. Godwin said that despite all the bad news, at least the *Manatee* and its crew and most of the other ships and their crews survived the storm.

Following all of this the Navy, of course, had its official investigation which could have resulted in the court-martial of Admiral Halsey. At any other time that may have been so. But the nation was at war and Halsey was considered the best officer they had to fight it. So, the consensus of the investigation was to put all this typhoon unpleasantness behind them and move forward in winning the war.

*   *   *

Turn now to Christmas Day 1944. For some reason (and he isn't telling), Godwin was assigned duty on that day on Mog Mog Island. His 'important' duty: picking up empty beer and soda pop bottles.

"While shipmates were undoubtedly enjoying a complete turkey dinner aboard ship, I had a canned spiced ham sandwich for lunch on Christmas Day," he said. "I'll never forget it. Certainly this was nothing to write home about. But what was cause to write home about was the fact that on that day I stood within 20 feet of Admiral Halsey and Admiral Nimitz—the top admirals in the Pacific theater of World War II."

Seeley said he spent 18 months on the *Manatee* during World War II. And during that time he saw the enemy only once. "A Japanese twin engine airplane came into view and we went to general quarters," he said. "She had us quite nervous, because we were afraid she was a Kamikaze plane. We had an escort carrier and she fired at her, but the plane got away."

Elsewhere, the year 1944 was noted by the Normandy invasion on June 6, the nomination of President Franklin D. Roosevelt for his fourth term, this time with Senator Harry S Truman of Missouri for the vice presidency. Then, in Europe, there was the Battle of the Bulge on December 16. Medically, however, it was the discovery of the antibiotic penicillin. It became known as the wonder drug that proved effective against wounds and a wide variety of infectious diseases. In addition, the use of the insecticide DDT was found to control and wipe out typhus.

*   *   *

Throughout January and February of 1945, the *Manatee* supported the forces then covering the Luzon landings in the Philippines. But on one of its wartime assignments, the *Manatee* departed from its task force and made its way through Surigao Straits and the Sulu Sea to a rendezvous where it joined the fleet in refueling operations. Heavy seas, however, made the task extremely difficult. Hoses and lines parted frequently and at times the bow of the battleship Wisconsin, taking fuel from the *Manatee*, was lifted clear out of the water by huge swells. Yet, despite the beating on everyone involved, the mission was completed successfully.

Next up was another war assignment. Now the ship was to return through the Sulu Sea and Surigao Strait to Ulithi, where it was to make preparations for the invasion of Iwo Jima. Picture the famous flag planted atop Mt. Suribachi. It's that Iwo Jima battle that would soon transpire. It wasn't easy.

It took the U.S. Marines 36 days of bitter and bloody fighting to secure the island. In the end, more than 4,000 Marines were killed and another 15,000 wounded. But for the Japanese it was much worse. They lost more than 20,000 men.

In support of the battle, the *Manatee* was on hand with not only oil, but by this time it was also supplying mail, aircraft belly tanks, depth charges, freight, motion pictures and a large number of personnel replacements.

At the end of February, the *Manatee* was ordered to return to Ulithi to pick up oil and then steam back to fuel the amphibious forces gathering for the Okinawa campaign. For the *Manatee* this trip was the first of a regular shuttle, picking up oil from Ulithi and delivering it to the carrier groups operating in the Battle of Okinawa.

Okinawa was a large island, about 60 miles long with four airfields. The Japanese had about 130,000 men here, about twice as many as had been expected. Yet while the Americans had lost heavily on land and at sea, on June 21, after 82 days of fighting,

21

the island was declared secure.

On July 2, the *Manatee* was ordered to provide support to carrier groups during planned strikes on the Japanese home islands. Moving at night for the rendezvous with the carriers, the *Manatee* refueled them within 200 miles of the enemy's coastline.

Fortunately, the plans to strike the Japanese homeland never had to take place. This was partly due to the dropping of two atomic bombs in August. But it was also due to the Soviet Army's invasion of Japanese-held Manchuria. Here the Soviets quickly defeated what was then the largest concentration of Japanese fighting forces. With the odds of winning now totally against them, the Japanese reluctantly agreed to end the conflict. The U.S. troops that did land on the Japanese mainland did so as occupiers. So, with the cessation of hostilities on August 15, the *Manatee* was ordered home, arriving in San Pedro, California on October 7.

*   *   *

In San Pedro there was liberty for the *Manatee* crew, of course, but there were also some days devoted to work. This included repairing and replacing broken parts and painting everything anew. It was on one of these painting assignments that *Manatee* Sailors Royce Godwin and George W. Smith were given the assignment to go over the side of the ship with buckets of paint and brushes. It was all to give it a good one-two.

Smith says he remembers it well. "Somehow Royce messed up the ropes, they tangled, loosened, and quickly dumped us over the side, right into the water below. We had a hell-of-a-time getting back aboard because we were laughing so hard."

Those fun times, however, were short lived. Within days the *Manatee* was back at sea, heading once again to the Western Pacific. By the end of November, the ship was actively supporting the occupation operations. A new captain was assigned. Captain R. G. Visser, on December 23, 1945, would replace Lieutenant Commander Joseph B. Smith at the helm of the *Manatee*.

In the end, 1945 was a monumental year. For not only did both Germany and Japan surrender, ending World War II, but it was the year atomic bombs were first used in warfare. The United Nations was launched, President Roosevelt died in office and Harry S. Truman became President of the U.S. And, as for the general public, the rationing of consumer products that was imposed during the war was lifted. For the most part, life was getting back to normal.

*   *   *

Keeping Your Real Name Is Often Not An Option

Manatee Sailors have long been given fitting nicknames which often described their characteristics like "Whitey", "Big Red" or "Shorty".

Some of the unusual nicknames were names like "Tamale", "Flip Flop" or "Pork Chop."

Many of these nicknames were kept under wraps due to them being part of evaluation reports and seen by only senior officers keeping track of the Sailor's mental well being. After all, you don't want totally unqualified officers with their hands on any trigger devices. It could start a war or something.

Recently some of these reports got out and they have been making the rounds. Here are a select few (minus the descriptive nicknames) originating from the United Kingdom Royal Navy.

- His men would follow him anywhere out of curiosity.
- Technically sound, but socially impossible.
- Since my last report he has reached rock bottom and has started to dig.
- This officer could go far – and the sooner he starts the better.
- This man is depriving a village somewhere of an idiot.

CHAPTER 2

1946-1947 AROUND
AND AROUND SHE GOES

Throughout 1946 and into 1947, the *Manatee* made three round trips between the oil ports on the Arabian Gulf and Tokyo. It was a time when spiraling inflation, acute shortage of housing and bitter labor disputes were facing Americans. On July 4, 1946, the Philippines were declared independent, now officially becoming the Republic of the Philippines. President Truman said he did this, keeping a promise made by the United States on acquiring the islands in 1898.

It was during this time period, in February 1946, when Robert D. Walton reported aboard. Walton was assigned as boat coxswain on the *Manatee's* 26-foot whale boat and 40-foot motor launches. Later on, he said, they added a LCVP. "We went to Inchon, Korea, emptied our tanks and had a three-day pass to Seoul," he said. "We then sailed to the Persian (Arabian) Gulf for a new cargo. We had liberties at Hong Kong, Singapore, Colombo, Ceylon (Sri -Lanka) and visited them again on our return trip."

All Sailors, regardless which ship they were assigned to, can relate to those liberty trips. When your ship was anchored in the harbor, which was often the case, rather than moored to a dock, going on liberty wasn't quite as easy. Small boats, attached to each ship, were launched to facilitate the crew's short trips to and from the shore.

Leaving the ship on liberty, everyone looks their best, clean and well-ironed clothes, squared away white hats and shined shoes. But it was on the way back that things would change just a bit. For most of the men, no longer are their clothes clean. No longer are their hats on straight, if on at all. Filled with whatever they drank at the local bars, for most of them it was a chore just to walk by themselves. Transporting these guys back to the ship, ac-

24

cording to Walton, was never an easy task.

"In Singapore three of our men took a vehicle that didn't belong to them and crashed it into a building," Walton said. "Of course they were arrested and jailed. My crew and I transported our executive officer and some other officers  to the police station. Here they would try to get them out of jail so we could be on our way to Iraq."

"We waited with our small boat tied to the pier for five hours," Walton said. "It took that long to talk the authorities into letting them go. And while the men didn't face charges in Singapore, the punishment aboard ship was severe. They lost some rank, were restricted to the ship for the duration of the cruise and had to sign up for another four-year hitch.

*   *   *

Enter now shipmate Tom Wheeler who served aboard the *Manatee* from 1946 to 1949. Wheeler said that in the 1940s the pay scale for Sailors wasn't much to shout about. But over-  seas travel, besides seeing the world, did have its perks that made up for it. One was the price of cigarettes aboard ship. "As I remember right," he said, "the price we paid in the ship's store was very reasonable, while on shore in places like Japan and the Philippians the price tag for those stogies was extreme to say the least. You can bet, whether we smoked or not, we took advantage of the potential profit. We became instant entrepreneurs.

"We used to stock up at sea and when we were in port we would have trade goods. The only problem we had was to get them legally off the ship and out the main gate without anyone catching on. We solved that by using cellophane tape, attaching each pack in strings of five packs. These strings of cigarette packs then would be attached to our legs. If we did it right we could get two cartons out in one trip."

*   *   *

Shipmate Walton said that although the *Manatee* was at sea for long periods of time, those liberty stops in ports, mostly in the Western Pacific were real treats. Other ports, such as in Ceylon and even China weren't the norm. And only once did he remember the *Manatee* visiting Iraq. He said that one time was when it was only Captain Visser and his staff who went ashore. They returned with several dignitaries who were invited for dinner.

After serving in the Western Pacific the *Manatee* sailed to Pearl Harbor in Hawaii. Here the ship would remain for a complete overhaul. For the crew it was a chance to get off the ship for a while. But unlike the tourist posters that depict the great life on the islands, there were few opportunities for Sailors on Oahu, at least, an island that you could drive completely around in a couple of hours. There was little time or funds to visit the other islands in the Hawaiian waters.

Over the years among the complaints about Hawaii were the high costs of almost everything. About the only thing a Sailor with limited funds could enjoy here was spending some time at the beach. Girl watching became an art form, but in those days the bikini hadn't been invented yet so a guy had to leave a lot to the imagination.

By September of 1947, with a new commanding officer, Captain James L. Shank, in charge, even this shore duty was to end when the *Manatee* was ordered back to the Arabian Gulf. On this voyage the ship was to travel through the Suez Canal, loading its oil at Ras Tanura, Arabia, and off-loading it at Norfolk, Virginia.

For Captain Shank, who served from March 26, 1947, to April 28, 1948, it wasn't an easy assignment because on November 13, in the midst of the Atlantic, a heavy storm hit, causing some damage to the ship's superstructure.

*   *   *

What Is It Like To Be In The Navy?

The one question Sailors get asked from time to time is , "What is it like to be in the Navy"? Depending on who you ask, the answer varies. Listed here are some of those responses.

* Buy a dumpster, paint it gray and live in it for six months straight. * In the middle of January, place a podium at the end of your driveway. Have your family stand watches at the podium, rotating four hour intervals. * Perform a weekly disassembly and inspection of your lawn mower. * Raise your bed to within six inches from the ceiling. * Repaint your entire house once a month. * Have your neighbor collect all your mail for a month, loosing every fifth item. * Have your five year old cousin give you a haircut with goat sheers. * When your children have been in bed for three hours, run into their room with a megaphone, and shout at the top of your lungs that your home is under attack, and order them to man their battle stations. * Post a menu on the refrigerator door informing your family that you are having steak for dinner. Then make them wait in line for at least an hour. When they finally get to the kitchen, tell them that you are out of steak, but you have hot dogs. Repeat daily.

Some Views From The Sky

Here are four different views from the air courtesy of the Naval Air Corps) of the Manatee at work or underway to far off destinations.

CHAPTER 3

1948 OFF TO SEE
THE WORLD... ALMOST

Early in 1948 the ship departed for the Persian (Arabian) Gulf and it was during this time that Captain H. W. Taylor took command of the *Manatee*.

For Tom Wheeler, being assigned to the not-so-glamorous *Manatee* was punishment from the word "go," but to rub matters in more was the fact he was assigned to the deck crew, a workhorse division if there ever was one.

"My discontent must have been showing because in time somehow I talked my way into the 4th Division Engineering Department," he said. "And lucky me I got the Engineer Log Room. With my Columbus system of typing (you know, find a key and land on it) and a dictionary I got by for the most of the three years I spent on the ship."

Wheeler said that for most of those years, memories of what happened are a little sketchy. But he said what he does remember, in detail, are those days visiting foreign ports. One such port visit was when the ship docked in Colombo, Ceylon (now Seri Lanka).

"Among the six of us who went ashore together that day was shipmate Doug Patterson. What we saw first was a line of snake charmers along the main street. So we talked one of them into telling us some of his secrets. And after much haggling we arrived at a fee.

"He told us that first you must catch a  cobra, small enough so that it would fit into a bushel basket. And oh, by the way, while he was telling us this he was also demonstrating it. So, continuing, he said you put the cobra in the basket and make sure the lid is firmly in place. Then you

30

raise the basket over your head and shake it with much vigor. Next you set the basket down in front of you, all the while getting your flute ready. At this point you start to weave sidewise, back and forth and back and forth again, all the while slowly taking the lid off the basket. Now you start to play the flute.

"Of course, as he did this the cobra started to rise slowly in the basket, transforming itself into that all-to-familiar hooded creature. He then stopped playing the flute, but kept on moving and said that the music means nothing. As long as I'm moving the snake will follow me. Now for the finale, he said, watch very closely and don't blink your eyes, or you'll miss all the action. We held our breath. He stopped moving and the snake nailed him straight on.

"At this point we thought that we would get out of paying the fee because surely this guy was not long for this world. But without blinking he took the basket lid and forced the snake back into the basket. He held out his hand, showing us the "bite" area. 'Do you think I'm crazy?' he asked. 'My cobra is defanged.'"

*　　*　　*

Wheeler said after all these years (he's 82 at this writing) he still has this fear of snakes. And it didn't help that night, not long after the snake charmer incident, that he was asleep in his bunk. Unbeknownst to him, a few of his "friends" bought a stuffed cobra which was permanently in the ready to strike pose. So, with Wheeler snoring away, they placed it resting on his open chest. Then, a little distance away, they made enough of a disturbance to awaken Wheeler. He opened his eyes, just enough, stared at the critter on top of him, yelled, brushed off the snake, and darted away in record time.

*　　*　　*

On another occasion, Wheeler and some Navy buddies were exploring the back country behind Colombo, Ceylon. They didn't see anyone around so they proceeded on the road into an area where a group of huts were located. But no sooner did they enter the area when an army jeep sped into the compound behind them. The jeep was loaded with Indian military police who proceeded to stop them. Then, less than politely, these policemen told them that they, in fact, had just entered a leper colony. Wheeler said there was no argument. The decision was unanimous. There was no more exploring the back-roads that day.

*   *   *

But Wheeler's most embarrassing moment came about when the *Manatee* made a liberty stop in Singapore. This time, dressed in a clean white uniform and with temperatures hovering well past 100 degrees, he went into town alone, thinking he would just get a cold beer.

"So here I am going into this very cool, almost cold, bar. I ordered a large UB beer, chugged it down real fast, waited several minutes and stepped out of the bar into that terrible heat," Wheeler said. "At this time Singapore had these open sewers on each side of the streets with crosswalks every eight to ten feet. Well, in my condition, I saw five of them crosswalks in one area and picked out what I thought was the middle one. Feeling no pain I aimed and started on my way, but missed the walkway entirely and stepped in, whatever it was, up to my belt-line, dress whites and all.

"I climbed out just as a Shore Patrol jeep was passing. The jeep stopped and gave me a hand—sort of. The trip, not inside mind you, but walking in front of the jeep all the way to the boat landing. Then, once at this location, I had to wait until the last liberty party was loaded and even then I sat in the bow while about 18 others sat near the stern. I stopped drinking beer and anything like it from that day forward."

*   *   *

Back in the states at that time the Truman Administration and Congress were fighting over the supposed presence of communists in government positions. The President largely ignored the warnings, calling one finding a "red herring." The scares, largely fanned by Senator Joseph McCarthy, wouldn't end until 1954 when he was exposed by the media and then censured by Congress for conduct unbecoming a Senator.

The Summer Olympics were held in London, England that year, the U.S. Open golf tournament was won by Ben Hogan and Citation became the eighth horse in history to win the Triple Crown.

All of this, of course, would be a world away for *Manatee's* Sailors who often would not hear of world events while at sea for long periods of time. The only changes would be the ocean itself. One day the waters would be choppy, the next smooth as glass and then extremely rough, the *Manatee* finding it difficult to keep on a compass setting.

All would agree that the most feared condition was the fog, because you never knew what was ahead of you. At times the fog was so thick you couldn't see ahead more than two feet. It was on one of these days, the fog pea-soup thick, that the story was told about the captain who ordered his ship's engines to stop. The ship was just going to stay calm until it was safe to move forward. After a long time a young Sailor on lookout said: "Sir, the sky is clear. I can see the heavens."

Without a beat the captain fired back: "Well, until the engines burst, we aren't going that way!"

It's true—in the *Manatee's* 30-year career, it never went that way. Where it did go on June 2, 1948, was Long Beach, California, arriving August 20, this time for a lengthy stay.

*   *   *

CHAPTER 4

1949-1950 A BIG CHANGE
FOR THE *MANATEE*

The year 1949 saw the formation of the North Atlantic Treaty Organization (NATO) which was formed with Belgium, Canada, Denmark, France, Great Britain, Italy, Iceland, Luxembourg, the Netherlands, Norway, Portugal, and the United States in tow.

The Hoover Commission found that many government enterprises were corrupt and inefficient. And a minimum wage bill was signed by President Truman, raising federal wages from 40 cents to 75 cents an hour.

All of those worldly matters, however, were left behind as the *Manatee* said goodbye once again to Long Beach on January 6, 1949. Aboard was a new skipper, Captain C. T. Corbin. And the orders now were to head for the Western Pacific where the ship would complete three round trip cruises between Sasebo, Japan, and the Persian (Arabian) Gulf.

William J. "Bill" Cress was aboard the *Manatee* at this time. And he remembered an incident that happened when the ship was anchored in a Formosa harbor.

"I was on watch on  the quarterdeck and about to get off when we received a message that there was a group who would soon be on their way to the states to play in the Softball Championship Games," he said. "What they needed was some practice and they wanted to know if some of our crew could be the opposing team. I put the word out that anyone wanting to play to report to the quarterdeck.

"It was a Sunday morning and hotter than blue blazes. I wasn't even sure we could get enough guys to make a team, but here they came, half asleep, some with no shirts, some with ball caps on backwards. It was a real rag tag group to say the least.

"We met the "champs" on a small island and couldn't believe our eyes. Here they were in smart uniforms, standard ball caps and all that, and most of us were looking like we couldn't even stand up straight. But after a rousing game and a few arguments in between innings, we beat them. I mean—really beat them! We never did find out how they fared in the tournament, if they went at all, after this stunning defeat."

*   *   *

Cress said that during his time in the Navy there were a number of memorable characters. Among his favorites was a *Manatee* Sailor named Bad Cobb. And yes, Cress said, that was his name.

"He was a full-blooded American Indian," Cress said. "He didn't read well so he had his shipmates read his mail to him. Among his letters were these notices from the Internal Revenue Service about income tax that was owed. Of course, Bad Cobb thought that because he resided on a reservation that he didn't have to pay. So he threw them all away.

"One day he brought me a notice to read to him. Again, it was from the IRS. The letter said it was the last time he would hear from them (they were going to take action). He said, 'Oh, good, then this is the last time I'll hear from them.' And so he tore the letter up and threw it away. None of us ever did find out if they caught up with him or not."

Cress said that although Bad Cobb had his problems, he could be counted on when you needed him. One example, he said, was when the *Manatee* crew was having trouble sending a line over to another ship at the beginning of a refueling operation.

"Time and again crewmembers tried, but each time failed to reach their mark. Everyone was angered and frustrated. Then someone remembered Bad Cobb. Where the bow and arrow came from I don't know, but they attached the line to it and he shot it over on the first try. Soon after a message from the other ship came through loud and clear: 'Who the hell is shooting arrows over here?'"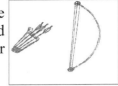

*   *   *

Ensign Robert W. Beard, who served on the *Manatee* from 1951 to 1953, reported for duty on September 27, 1951. Beard said he remembered Bad Cobb as among the best liked and respected members of the crew. As a full-blooded member of the Sioux tribe, Beard said he was a strikingly powerful-looking man in his mid-30s who didn't talk much and didn't smile. He said he looked every bit the part of the stereotypical American Indian.

 "What he was, however," Beard said, "was greatly affected by firewater and when under its influence, no one wished to incur his wrath. Even the officers treated him with special care. I remember once he asked for a 10-day leave to attend a pow-wow which was granted. But when he returned back from that leave the quarterdeck log reported nothing to the fact he was several days late. He was, however, on orders of the captain, to be escorted directly to the captain's cabin.

"Knowing full well he was late, the captain merely asked, ' how was the pow wow?'"

The reply: "Great."

Then the captain said, "Nice to have you back."

His reply: "Thank you."

"And that was it," Beard said. "Now should anyone else report back from leave several days late it would be you-know-what to pay. But not Bad Cobb. He was an island unto himself."

*   *   *

On July 17, 1949, the ship was back in California, but this time in San Francisco, awaiting something no one expected. It was a complete conversion into a different kind of vessel. Her rig for fueling at sea was removed and the *Manatee* began 20 months' service as a MSTS vessel (Military Sea Transportation Service).

The *Manatee* was now basically a cargo ship, able to transport not only various supplies, but ammunition and infantry troops as well. President Harry S. Truman ordered the transformation, not only for the *Manatee*, but for numerous other ships. It was to fill a critical need for cargo vessels at the time.

At first the *Manatee* was put to work along the West Coast, and then the Caribbean was added, as was the Gulf and East Coasts. Throughout most of 1950 she made four trips to Norfolk via the Panama Canal and the Dutch West Indies. Then, on October 27, she departed Boston for Ras Tanura on the Persian (Arabian) Gulf. Before the cruise ended she had called on Manila, the Philippines, Yokosuka, Japan and Pearl Harbor. After that the captain pointed the ship west. She was heading home.

*   *   *

A rare formal presentation, like this one in 1966, was held to recognize *Manatee* Sailors when they performed beyond their duties.

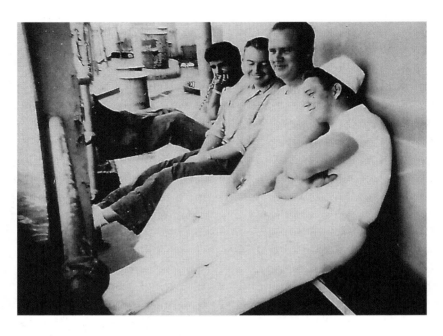

38

LEFT: At sea on the Manatee in 1953 are, from left, Jose (Little Joe) Padilla, Marty Montgomery, shipmate Brinkley and shipmate Ridgeway. RIGHT: Brian M. Vesper is shown with two other shipmates. BELOW LEFT: While one does the work, another supervises. BELOW RIGHT: At sea work party (that means work - yes, party - no)

Work, Rest & Those In-betweeners

CHAPTER 5

1950-1951 NO MORE FUNNY BUSINESS

Someone in the Navy Department thought enough was enough for the *Manatee* to be disguised as an MSTS vessel. So, they took out a bunch of things and added some things and before you knew it, the *Manatee* was back into its original form as an oil tanker.

All of this might have had something to do with the nasty things going on in Korea at the time, with communist forces in the North making moves on the anti-communist forces in the South. This came to a head on June 25, 1950. It was then that North Korean troops and tanks crossed the 38th Parallel into South Korea. It marked the beginning of the Korean War.

As might have been predicted, the *Manatee* was back into the thick of things, arriving in Japanese waters on March 17, three months before the shooting war started. After brief periods at Tokuyama and Sasebo, she received orders to replenish ships patrolling in the Formosa Strait, returning to Sasebo May 20.

By the time the United Nations voted to help South Korea and had appointed General Douglas MacArthur Commander in Chief of the UN Command, the North Koreans were already well inside South Korea. So, to speed things up a bit, the first American troops were airlifted in from Japan. Then the war became a struggle between the Americans and the North Koreans for Pusan, the only remaining good harbor in South Korea. And the *Manatee* was right there, servicing the Navy's ships in combat areas off the Korean coast.

*   *   *

Boatswain's Mate Third Class Max Bryant was aboard the *Manatee* and assigned to the Second Division at that time. He said among the things he remembered well was when the Captain W.

G. Chapple, got himself in more than a little bit of trouble. Chapple served from August 1, 1950, to November 7, 1951.

"What a great guy this captain was," Bryant said. "But I think he was a little disappointed that he wasn't on a warship just to be a part of the real action. I remember one time he had the *Manatee* going in real close to the Korean shore, the object being to turn the *Manatee's* 'big guns' on the enemy."

Other accounts said that while Chapple was thinking just how best to accomplish the task the destroyers and cruisers were already shelling gun emplacements ashore. Chapple, accounts said, decided to back the *Manatee* around towards shore, and while this was taking place, he ordered the stern 5-inch gun manned. Within a few minutes he began to fire on a rice paddy, trying to hit a small bamboo shed. The *Manatee's* shells exploded instead over a large area of rice fields, terrifying the Koreans but failing to hit the target.

The *Manatee's* guns were designed mostly for self-protection and mostly for up-close use. So, of course, the ship's small (in comparison) guns were no match up against the really big guns attached to destroyers, cruisers and battleships. But accounts said, Captain Chapple didn't care, He was going to give it the one-two anyway.

A former submarine skipper, Captain Chapple sought every opportunity to have himself and his *Manatee* crew look good. One example of this was recorded when the ship made a stop at Keelong, Formosa. Here he convinced the press not only to interview a few of his most outstanding crewmembers, but to write flattering articles concerning the fine conduct of his men on liberty.

Back now to the battle taking place on the Korean shore. Bryant said that while the captain was busy with the "enemy," he got this frantic call from the admiral on a battleship several miles to our rear. "The battleship, of course, was ready to give the shoreline some heavy bombardment of its own," Bryant said. "And as I remember it, this admiral had some sharp words to say. In essence it was (expletives deleted): 'Get the hell out of the way or I'll blow you out of the water!'"

Ship Fitter Third Class John Vaughan, who was also on board at the time, said he remembered that the admiral in question was none other than Admiral Arleigh Burke, the World War II hero. He said the battleship came at the *Manatee* at flank speed and then some.

Admiral Burke

"I believe the engineers must have wired the safety valves down as they passed our port side about a quarter-of-a-mile away. It was so close that we took water over the well deck. We could do nothing but watch in amazement. As the battleship slowed to a near stop, we caught up with it and watched as the battleship's 16-inch shells were fired in rapid succession toward the coast. Before all the commotion, the enemy had units of our forces pinned down. Now they were free to make their move.

As far as the *Manatee* was concerned, Bryant said that despite the captain's "trouble" he retired several years later as an admiral, and died several years after that.

Bryant was just 17 years old when he joined the Navy in 1946 and got out in 1950. It was due to the Korean War that he was called back into the service and assigned to the *Manatee*.

On September 15, with a stalemate on the ground, MacArthur made a daring amphibious landing at Inchon, over 200 miles in the rear of the North Korean advance units attacking Pusan. By this time, however, the *Manatee* had already been in the South Korean waters for five months and had returned to Long Beach Aug. 11. Here it would stay for the next seven months.

*   *   *

Vaughan said that while the wartime experiences on the *Manatee* were burned into his memory, one incident stateside also had a lasting impression. It was during this period when the *Manatee* was in Long Beach that a group of *Manatee* Sailors traveled to a bar in nearby San Pedro.

"At first there was nothing unusual about the trip," he said. "A few of the boys and I were just going over to this bar to have a beer. Once we were there this heavily endowed woman of American Indian descent came over and sat down next to us. It seemed as one of the guys knew her and asked her to show all of us her tattoos.

"Of course, most of us weren't at all interested, until she spread her legs and pulled up her skirt. The first thing we noticed is that she didn't have on any underwear. Then those who expressed no interest before, now took notice. But it wasn't over yet. There on the inside of her thigh was a tattoo that simply read 'Pay As You Enter.'"

*   *   *

On November 7 a change of command ceremony was held aboard the *Manatee* in Long Beach Naval Shipyard. Commander J. C. McGoughran relieved Captain Chapple of his duties as commanding officer. That evening the crew hosted a going-away party for their now former captain, the skipper who led them safely through their one big "battle" in Korea.

By the end of 1951, the world was hovering close to the brink of a world war. All of this came about because Chinese Communist troops had entered the Korean campaign. To counter this, General MacArthur asked for permission to strike into Chinese territory.

But this was seen by the Truman Administration as tantamount to declaring war on China. Because China had an alliance with the USSR, it would mean major consequences to all concerned. The United Nations quickly and strongly suggested that the U.S. not attack Chinese bases. In the end, the United States stood with the UN. This, of course, was welcome news to the American public. Tempers at home were already getting short as casualties in Korea had reached 100,000 and there was no end in sight.

CHAPTER 6

1952 AROUND AND AROUND SHE GOES

The *Manatee* remained in port for the first few months in 1952. But it was back to the business at hand on March 21, 1952. It was then that the ship once again said goodbye to the states for its next deployment to the Western Pacific.

It was on this cruise that *Manatee* Radarman Second Class Farroll Barrett remembered shipmate, John Lott. Standing just five foot eight inches tall and weighing a mere 125 pounds, Lott seemed to be the kind of guy that certainly wouldn't pick a fight. But Barrett said all of this was deceiving.

"Lott and I reported aboard the *Manatee* at the same time and we became fast friends—for a while," Barrett said. "He had done some amateur boxing before the Navy and was feisty to say the least. On a couple of occasions in Sasebo we did liberty together with a couple other guys and I learned quickly that after a couple of those 25 ounce Asahi beers, he liked to start trouble. And, to make matters worse, he always went after the biggest guy he could find. Sure enough, we all ended up in a brawl.

"On the last liberty, I and another shipmate Lynn Miller had with him, we got separated during the course of the evening. It wasn't long before a fight broke out a ways away. I recall telling Lynn I bet John was in the middle of it. We got closer and sure enough he was into it with a guy bigger than himself.

"The guy had him on the ground working him over pretty good. Stupid me: I pulled the guy off him and then bent over to help my friend get up. While he was getting up my friend swung with an uppercut that caught me flush in the mouth, loosening a tooth. I went down bleeding all over my whites while others in the general melee stepped on me a few times.

"Needless to say, it was the last time I went on liberty with John. And, to remind me of this misadventure is that to this day, I still have a small scar inside my upper lip where it busted open."

*   *   *

Barroom brawls were not all that uncommon for many *Manatee* crew members. But they certainly didn't have exclusive rights to the rituals. Just ask William J. "Bill" Cress, who served on the *Manatee* from 1948 to 1954.

"We were in Hong Kong and there was this British ship, a destroyer, there as well," he said. "I was in charge of our Shore Patrol operating out of a British police station. We had a call that there was a riot at a local bar. When we got there, the place was in shambles and we got in the midst of the fighting. One Brit had a table leg pounding the juke box screaming, 'It's a lie! It's a bloody lie!'

"When we got things calmed down and sorted out, this is what we were told happened. They were all drinking and talking amicably when one of the 'Yanks' put money in the juke box and selected '*The Battle of New Orleans*.' Of course, in those days you could understand every word in a song. So they all heard the line that went like this: 'We fired our guns and the British started running down the Mississippi to the Gulf of Mexico. We fired again and they continued running down the Mississippi to the Gulf of Mexico.' That, of course, was all it took to get the Brits riled up and the fighting to begin."

*   *   *

Cress said he had two nicknames while aboard the *Manatee*. The first was "Ace." He explains it this way:

"We were in the harbor and aboard the ship in Japan when the admiral, aboard another ship that was leaving port, sent a 75-word message by signal light for our captain. I was on the light and kept it on while receiving the message. When you keep the light on it means you are receiving. I got the message right away, without asking for any repeats, and delivered it to our captain. It was a letter of commendation for the excellent service the *Manatee* had provided.

"From that day forward the guys in my division started calling me 'Ace.' Of course it was only a matter of time before the rest of the crew joined in as well."

The nickname lasted only until Cress got himself another moniker. And here's how "Ace" turned into "Sarge."

*   *   *

"While in the Navy and on board the *Manatee* I received a letter from my local draft board at home saying I was to report to them within 10 days or they would take action," he said. "We were off the coast of Korea at the time and when I told Commander Huntley about it he asked if he could reply.

"In his letter he said something to the effect that I was currently in a job working for my 'uncle' who provided me with a uniform, meals, room and transportation. He had me working out of the states (overseas). The letter was so worded that it was amusing. Someone from the draft board replied saying that they had received all kinds of excuses to their letters, but never one that was

46

so original and funny. They wished me luck. As a result, aboard the ship, I was from that day forward called 'Sarge.'"

Whatever fun times the *Manatee* Sailors had, however, didn't last long. For all too soon it was back to the business at hand—supporting all those ships still engaged in the Korean War.

*   *   *

But while the war waged on, it didn't prevent other events from occurring. Dan Mehner remembers when all hands weren't paying attention like they should have been and the *Manatee* rammed into a smaller ship. It wasn't, of course, an enemy ship, at least not before this incident. "The *Manatee*, seeing an imminent collision, put itself in full reverse. We were all shaking and shaking even more when the ships collided," he said. "The *Manatee* had little damage, the other ship was not so lucky.

"If that wasn't enough, there was another incident when a seaman cook came off shore duty a wee bit intoxicated, picked up a knife and stabbed another shipmate in his leg. Needless to say he didn't pass go, but went directly into the ship's brig."

*   *   *

All too soon it was back to the work at hand. But those refueling-at-sea operations weren't entirely a chore. When carriers were alongside they would sometimes have a military band on hand to serenade the *Manatee* crew. The *Manatee* in turn would sometimes put on a record and with loudspeakers pointed toward the receiving ships, serenade them in return.

For nearly a week, however, the *Manatee* had a surprise in store—particularly for the carriers who liked to show off their full-fledged bands. On board the *Manatee* for five days was the entire 7th Fleet Band, without a question the Navy's, if not the entire military's, finest. The crews of the other ships, not knowing it was the famous band playing before their eyes, marveled

47

at how the *Manatee*, with such a small crew, could be so musically talented.

*   *   *

Nobody for a moment forgot, however, that there was a war going on. So, needless to say, shipmates were a little edgy. But in the summer, when the compartments were so hot you'd think you were in a sauna, things had to give. Like the time Machinist Mate Second Class Eldon Gard said he couldn't take it anymore. And wartime or not he was going to take his pillow and blanket and move topside.

"It was a pleasure sleeping on the deck on those really nice nights," he said. "I'll never forget one such night, however. I was sleeping soundly when I was startled awake by the engines of an oncoming airplane. It was flying straight at where I was sleeping, totally getting my attention and scaring the #$%& out of me. Fortunately," Gard said, "the plane turned skyward," not only missing the *Manatee*, but more important for Gard, missing him as well.

*   *   *

For some reason all of the enemy planes the *Manatee* faced over the years, none actually fired on the ship. Sometimes, however, there were unforeseen situations. Jim Todd, a fire control technician and who served aboard the ship from 1950 to 1953, remembers one of those occurrences.

"We were off North Korea and were called to general quarters because the lookouts sighted two Russian MiGs coming in fast. I was a gun director for the three-inch guns and was watching that the gun crew was ready. But when the gunners mate dropped the gun breech a fifth of whiskey came sliding out of the barrel. Luckily, the hot shell-man very delicately caught the valuable liquid before it hit the deck."

48

Todd said that with no shots fired from either side, the *Manatee* crew went back to whatever they were doing before, as if nothing was amiss. As for what happened to that fifth of whisky? That still remains a mystery.

*   *   *

One never knew, of course, just what kind of a situation the ship would get itself into. So it had to be constantly preparing for an emergency. And Yeoman First Class Sam Hartley, who was serving on the ship at that time, will never forget one such "preparation."

"It was early in 1952," he said. "We were out of the fuel docks at Sasebo, Japan, under a full load of oil and other fleet supplies, including fleet mail and some ship's replacement Sailors. We were running alone but under escort by a friendly patrol craft forward from the Republic of Korea and two small Thailand escorts to our sides. Then, somewhere in the Korean Strait, the skipper called for a gunnery practice.

"The gunners had painted an empty oil drum yellow and tossed it over board as a floating target. The *Manatee* circled the drum at a distance, allowing the various 20mm and 40mm deck mounts to fire at the target.

"The drum was still afloat when our practice ended, so the skipper asked the three small escort ships, one at a time, to come in and hold gun action on the float. Instead of following us in our circle, the Republic of Korea escort moved in on the opposite side of the drum from our circling position and started popping away at the drum with a rapid fire deck gun.

"My first sea duty during my other Navy enlistments included World War II sub duty. In an emergency dive, we could clear the bridge and have the conning tower under water in between 30 and 60 seconds. But the *Manatee* did one better this day.

"I was the captain's talker on the *Manatee* bridge and I want to tell you when that other ship started shooting in our direction, the

49

starboard wing of the bridge was cleared faster than any crash dive I ever experienced. And I thought the sub Sailors were good!

"As the shooting began we all ran for cover, every man for himself, with the skipper yelling over his shoulder at the radioman with ship-to-ship communications, 'CEASE FIRE! CEASE FIRE!'"

As it turned out no *Manatee* Sailor was hurt and there was no damage to the ship. But Hartley said that he felt every Sailor on board believed every round was personal.

*   *   *

The *Manatee*, of course, wasn't meant to be in the heat of battle, only to be nearby in case one that was in the fighting needed something. Unfortunately, nobody told that to the enemy as Seaman Apprentice William C. Bergmeister, just out of Class 'A' School, discovered all too soon.

"During the 1952 cruise in October the *Manatee* became part of a battle flotilla," he said. "While we were rerouted to an invasion somewhere on the east coast of Korea, the entire crew was under Condition III watches, four hours on and four hours off.

"When the ship was in Condition III, my assignment was the forward port side 3-inch gun. There were about six of us in that gun tub. One of us had to man binoculars. Suddenly we observed three tiny, shiny specks of jet planes high in the sky. Since they were shiny, not blue, we assumed they were U.S. Air Force planes.

"Not so. The PA announced general quarters—enemy aircraft at 12 o'clock. And when the regular general quarters gun crew arrived on station, I headed to my damage control assignment aft of the cargo deck, port side.

"After breaking out hoses and dogging down portholes and hatches, I had only to stand and watch as the jet fighters began a long dive. By now our guns were under automatic fire control and were following the planes down in unison. When it appeared the planes were in range, they suddenly veered to starboard.

"There was a collective sigh of relief from everyone. But it didn't last. Within a minute or two the PA announced 'enemy aircraft approaching at 3 o'clock,' and we were on edge once again.

"The next thing we knew was that the planes were in full view—approaching fast, just above the waves. Again our guns depressed to meet the enemy planes. And again the aircraft pulled away to their right. And off they went once again, this time never to return."

Bergmeister said the crew was certainly relieved, but didn't understand why the planes didn't attack a sitting target like the *Manatee* with its full load of very flammable oil and jet fuel. Within minutes, he said, everyone found out why.

"It seemed like they came out of nowhere—American destroyers to our left and right and the heavy cruiser *Los Angeles*, which came close by our port side. Those enemy planes probably saw those ships approaching long before we did and didn't want to get caught in a bad situation."

*   *   *

Manatee Seaman Dan Mehner said he remembers just the opposite. Rather than the enemy disappearing, he said he remembers the day when the U.S. forces disappeared. "We were traveling as a task force," he said. "There were destroyers all around us. There were cruisers, all kinds of ships, in fact. This went on for days. Every time we would look out, U.S. naval ships were everywhere."

He said he went about doing his own thing, feeling safe, even in a war zone, when he again looked up. "I couldn't believe my eyes," he said. "I looked east, then west, south, then north. No sign of any ships anywhere. The *Manatee* was totally alone, and by the way, vulnerable to an enemy attack."

What happened? Where did these ships go? Mehner said he never did find out.

*   *   *

If you say storekeeper on a Navy ship, one might think it's the person who watches over the candy bars and soda pop in the ship's commissary, even consuming, or rather, checking out the merchandise from time to time. But storekeeper Bergmeister said his duties were a little more far-reaching than that. And it included a title—The Ullage King. This is the person who inventories the fuel cargo before and after fuel is pumped to other ships. In other words—a gas station attendant who doesn't do windows. In 1952 the fuel carried on the *Manatee* consisted of aviation gasoline, diesel fuel, jet fuel and black oil (Navy special fuel oil or NSFO).

*   *   *

At the end of June the *Manatee* arrived in Takau, Formosa, relieving another so-called sea cow as station vessel. Here, in the Formosa Straits the *Manatee* provided not only fuel but food, mail and passengers to a variety of ships on patrol. But beyond that, this one time the *Manatee* served a diplomatic mission as hosts to the Chinese Nationalist Armed Forces.

Virtually all of her high-ranking officers were aboard as observers in the Formosa Straits maneuvers—serious stuff. But, when this was all over what followed was swimming, baseball and basketball parties. Most popular, however, was boxing. A team from the *Manatee* competed with the Chinese-Formosa boxing team, with one of the matches having well over 3,000 Chinese in attendance. Needless to say, any rooting for the *Manatee* team was totally drowned out by her opponents.

*   *   *

Toward the end of 1952, the ship once again returned to California. This time it was to San Pedro and Todd's civilian shipyard. Here the *Manatee* remained for repairs and the installation of some safety features.

What the *Manatee* Sailors discovered in 1952 was that life on the home front wasn't quite the same. It was a year of flying saucer sightings in night skies all across the nation. The Air Force even published photographs of the unidentified objects, and virtually everyone believed they were manned by emissaries from outer space.

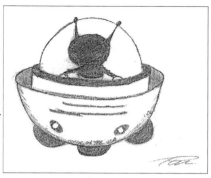

Male college students had their eyes on something else—the girl dorms. No sooner had one college participated in so-called panty raids, the others followed. It went something like this: A delegation from the boys dorms would "attack" the girl sorority houses demanding as ransom articles of feminine underclothing. Of course, there was no argument, and the girls freely surrendered what was required.

*   *   *

Many *Manatee* Sailors looked forward to the eating experience when offered on the fantail of the ship, like this one in 1966. A reminder of those barbeques back home.

Today (1962) It's All Work And No Play

Everyone on board has assigned duties during refueling operations. Sending messages (TOP) is one and manning a winch (BELOW) is another. Once the oil starts to flow (RIGHT) there's a little waiting and watching to make sure all is going as planned.

CHAPTER 7

1953 SOME SLEEPLESS NIGHTS

After the *Manatee* crew had settled down from celebrating New Year's Eve and welcoming the New Year in 1953, someone was buried in paperwork, ordering new supplies for the *Manatee's* next cruise to the Western Pacific. The crew didn't know about it at the time but soon found out that all was not well. Storekeeper William Bergmeister explained what happened next.

"Part of the provisions turned out to be the captain's favorite snack food, pickled pigs feet. The only problem was that the warehouse misread the requisition for 50 pounds as 5,000 pounds. The pigs' feet came in cardboard cartons containing glass jars. When the cartons were slid down a ladder, almost all of the jars broke. What a mess! You can probably guess the loss was charged to the enlisted men's mess. And to make up for the cost, many a meal after that contained a good share of Navy beans."

*   *   *

Bergmeister said, however, that was only the beginning of the *Manatee's* problems at that time. "During our voyage back to the Far East, somewhere between Hawaii and Japan, the *Manatee* endured extreme sea conditions. Waves were forty to fifty feet high, all from a distant storm," he said.

"Movement on weather decks was restricted and permission to go forward was required from the bridge. The provisions bulk storeroom was in the bow area and I had to go forward to break out food. While moving forward I stopped behind the bridge superstructure to check wave action. When I got out onto the forward catwalk, I saw a big wave coming. I held onto the pipe railing with both hands and was engulfed in a giant wave. My hat was gone but I ran to the forward hatch before the next one hit. It was not a fun time.

"During the storm, several rivets popped along the seam where tank number five on the starboard side was located. The fuel in the tank was contaminated and as a result the contents in that tank weren't able to be used. The unstableness of the rivets was the biggest concern. Our engineering officers, Lieutenant Benson and Ensign Potter had thought of the possibility that the ship just might split into two parts. In the end, the *Manatee* stood the test."

*   *   *

One of the most important jobs on any ship is that of the navigator. The job involves continually keeping track of the ship's position and to plot how best to get from point A, where it is at the moment, to point B, it's final destination. The main principles of navigation haven't changed much over the centuries. It goes back to when those ancient Greeks and seafaring Vikings did their maneuvering solely by checking the positions of the sun and stars. Today we have such helps as sextants and chronometers, among other gadgets.

But even in the mid-1950s, when the duty of ship's navigator fell to Ensign Robert W. Beard, navigation was still a chore. Beard, who wrote a book about his two years aboard the *Manatee*, explained some of the challenges he faced in navigation. His book, *Astride The Sea Cow*, addressed the subject this way:

"Finding one's location on the globe seems like a simple matter," he wrote. "Plot your starting position on a chart, adjust it for the course, speed, and time travel, and there's where you are."

He wrote that this is called "dead reckoning." But, he added, there were also other considerations. "Among them," he wrote, "were currents and weather and steering errors. Then," he wrote, "there was fouling on the ship's hull that alters your course and speed, especially over long distances. And if that wasn't problematic enough," he added, "that there was no way to determine *Manatee*'s speed except by counting the turns of her propellers, and converting propeller turns into a vessel's speed depended on her loading and trim." If all this sounds confusing, well, it is. But somehow in the 30 some years *Manatee* was on duty, the navigators never got the ship or its crew lost on the high seas.

*   *   *

As anyone who served aboard a ship knows, ship's captains can be conceived as being a little bit troublesome or downright irritating at times. It was one of those times that Lieutenant Junior Grade James H. Hardy, the communications officer, remembers vividly. And it all happened following the worst of this storm, but still amid a heavy weather situation. Here's how he tells it.

"A requirement of the Navy is the filing of a 'movement report' in order to keep the area commander informed of your location. Also, as part of the report, an estimated time of arrival (ETA) of the ship at the next port was required," Hardy said.

"This particular morning we were running in heavy weather as we were several days out of Sasebo, Japan, our ultimate destination. It was obvious that our speed of advance was going to be significantly less than we had predicted earlier. This meant the filing of an amended movement report.

"The Captain J. C. McGoughran, was up on the bridge, as was I, the quartermaster, the helmsman, the port and starboard lookouts, the officer of the deck, the navigation officer in the back room, and the messenger. The captain sent word via the messenger for Kirk Sperry, the operations officer, to report to the bridge. Sperry was deeply engrossed in his work down below and was mildly annoyed at the abrupt interruption...

"Yes, captain," he said on arriving on the bridge.

"Say, Sperry, we've got to get out a corrected movement report, telling these people that we are going to be late."

"Well captain, how fast do you want to go?"

"Oh…I don't know – what do you think?"

"Well, how about 10 knots. The original report was based on about 15 knots. Ten knots will get us there at 0800 on the Seventh."

"No…no…that's much too fast. You know we couldn't possibly hold that speed in this sea. Look Sperry, you should know these things. Get the dope and figure it out for about five knots."

Kirk disappeared and after about 15 minutes he emerged from the chart room with his solution.

"What's the dope Sperry? When will we arrive?"

"At that speed, captain, we should make Sasebo about 1000 on the ninth."

"Oh no, no, that's too late. Can't we do better than that?"

"Well, how fast do you want to go, captain?"

"Oh…try 6.2 knots. When does that put us in?"

Sperry left for another session in the chart room, and returned to the bridge.

"That will get us into Sasebo 4 o'clock in the morning of the ninth."

"That's no good. Look Sperry, you know we can't go into that harbor at night. Try some other speed."

"Well, captain, how fast do you think you can go?"

"Try 7.3 knots."

"OK."

Sperry disappeared again. When he returned this time he looked a little less lively and his words were short, his comments cryptic.

"When do we get into Sasebo?"

"1500 on the eighth."

"Hmmm…well…I'd like to get in there earlier, if I could."

"How fast do you want to go, captain?"

"Get us into Sasebo early in the morning." Sperry disappeared. Fifteen minutes passed. Sperry reappeared, crossed the bridge, and made a grimace to the navigator, who responded with a knowing smile.

"Eight point four knots gets us into Sasebo at 0400 the morning of the eighth."

"Well, you know, that's pretty early in the morning; I wonder if we couldn't get there the night before. That would give us an extra day."

"Captain," Kirk said meekly, "there's one thing you can't change, and that's the distance we have to go. How fast do you want to go?"

"See if you can't get us in there the evening before."

Kirk disappeared into the chart room again. When he returned the captain saw him and said, "Hasn't that message gone out yet? That damned thing was priority and should have gone out long ago. What have you been doing? What am I supposed to do, run a kindergarten for navigators?"

"If we make nine knots we can get to Sasebo at 1900 the evening of the seventh."

"That's no good. We've got to get there in the morning because we will have a lot of work to do. Now get us there in the morning."

Sperry left, but returned quite soon.

"Ten knots will get us there at 0800 on the seventh, captain."

"That's more like it, why didn't you say that in the first place?"

Hardy said the message went out "...Speed of advance 10 knots...estimate time of arrival 0800 seven February..."

"Unfortunately," he said, "for the communications officer (me) the message was followed 12 hours later by a second missive "... speed of advance (SOA) last 12 hours 4 knots. SOA uncertain. ETA uncertain...will advise."

*　　　*　　　*

Seaman Claude T. Davis, who reported aboard the *Manatee* just before it left on this mission, had survived the storm with everyone else. But what he remembers the most now, is not the storm but one other experience that repeated itself over and over—so he couldn't forget. Here is how he describes the scene:

"The amidships compartment was quiet except for the usual nighttime sounds. An eerie glow from red night lights bathed over the sleeping forms. Ah, such peaceful rest after a busy day at sea. Men stirred as dreams of home or that last liberty port drifted through their subconscious minds.

"The watch in the radio shack was busy with incoming messages. Dispatches were quickly sent to the bridge where things were set in motion. Somewhere a task force was in need of fuel and was headed our way. The crew slept on. A rendezvous was set and course changes were made for first light. Still the crew slept on.

"Down in the berthing area the dreams went on—and then—sometime around 0430 a sound broke into the peacefulness of blissful sleep. Not much at first, just a tiny click. A gentle snap; now it gets a little louder. A groan, a pop, snap, groan, SNAP, POP, POP. Men start to stir, stretch and sit up on the sides of their bunks. Some wander off to the head; others start to dig out their cleanest dirty clothes. That sound is steam coming up on deck. Everybody knows that means an early reveille. Somebody needs fuel and somebody is going to give it to them—that somebody is going to be us!"

Not quite over just yet, Davis said what he next heard was a blast on the PA system: "Now reveille! reveille! Up all hands! Man your special sea and refueling stations! All hands on deck!"

Davis continued, "The fresh morning air starts the blood to flow. Booms are hoisted and made fast, messenger lines flaked out on deck, phone lines made ready and hoses swinging in the saddle lines. The sound of water rushing over the well deck. The smell of salt air in your nose. Now I know why I left the farm—I just love this #@%$!!!"

*   *   *

Despite the work aboard ship, there were moments of wonder in seeing parts of the world one may never see again. One of these was a two-week journey east from Pearl Harbor to a stop at Kwajalein Atoll in the Marshall Islands. In January of 1944, it was the site of one of the most intense battles in the Pacific in World War II. It took the lives of many Americans, but even more, 3,000 and counting Japanese soldiers. And even though in the early 1950s the war had been over for a good decade, you wouldn't know it. For the *Manatee* crew was able to still see debris from that battle lying about the beaches. It included landing craft, trucks, and jeeps, all rusting and beyond repair.

Next stop was Midway, the site of another massive World War II battle. A small island consisting of just two-and-a-half square miles, its importance in the war was undeniable. On this visit, however, the *Manatee* crew was focusing on something else. Gooney birds. That's right. Crewmembers had seen all  those nature documentaries. The buffalo and antelope herds, the alligators, the timber wolves. But there also were those strange, almost goofy birds—the gooneys. And here, at Midway, is where they lived.

A large sea bird, the gooney was known for its awkwardness. Being less than graceful was far too kind for these members of the albatross family. Taking flight was one thing, but it was their landings that put them in the comic books. It never failed; each landing was a spectacle of tumbles, feathers and feet flying in all directions. But despite their difficulties, they made it every time.

*   *   *

On April 18, it was time once again for a change in command on the *Manatee*. A ceremony was held in Sasebo, Japan, when Commander F. A. Brock relieved Commander McGoughran as *Manatee's* skipper.

At that time the pattern for the *Manatee* was to spend a month with the Taiwan Straits Patrol and the remainder of the tour operating out of Sasebo, Japan in support of the Korean operations.

The pattern also included the participation in fleet operations and in underway training exercises. The only breaks occurred when the *Manatee* crew was offered some shore time when the ship underwent its regular overhauls.

*   *   *

One *Manatee* Sailor who remembers one particular shore time well is Radarman Second Class Farroll Barrett. It was in mid-1953 when the ship arrived in Kaohsiung, a natural protected harbor on the southwestern tip of the island of Formosa.

"We were designated station ship for 30 days. During that time I had a couple of weeks of shore patrol duty and we would go ashore a couple of hours before regular liberty commenced for the various ships in the harbor.

"Part of our duty was to make the rounds of the bars and clubs to establish a relationship with the management, and of course, the hostesses. I became enamored of a cute little gal in one of the clubs, and for two weeks, tried to get her to take me home with her with no luck.

"On the night before we were to leave for two weeks' R & R in Hong Kong, she decided it was time. The *Manatee* was to get underway at 0600 the next morning and I woke up with no idea where I was at about 0530. She got me a three wheel bike carriage and in the rush to get to the fleet landing, I could not find my jumper or my shoes. No matter, off we went."

"When we got to the landing the ship had just gotten underway, perhaps moving at three or four knots. Fortu-

nately, it was not a long distance from the landing to the ship, and I got into a bumboat yelling and waving my arms while the boat man oared as fast as he could towards the ship.

"Someone on the ship saw and heard me and they actually stopped and waited for us to get there. The Jacobs ladder came over the side from the well deck, and I climbed on board sans shoes and jumper, looking and feeling not too good.

"Needless to say I was soon attending captains' mast while underway to Hong Kong. I was pretty lucky as I kept my rating, however, I was docked some pay and restricted to the ship the two weeks we were in Hong Kong."

*　　*　　*

If Barrett's experiences weren't frightening enough, another *Manatee* Sailor, Theron Gailey, a Yeoman Second Class, said he had an experience as well that he hasn't forgotten.

"It was in April of 1953, and we had just left Sasebo, Japan, for a firing practice in the Sea of Japan," he said. "Our escort ship at this time was the HTMS *Tachin* (PF-1) from Thailand. The engineering officer and his chief petty officer and I were to go aboard the *Tachin* as observers of the operation.

"On the morning of our scheduled departure the weather had become quite turbulent, and our carrying out the exercise was questionable. After waiting around for a while, the decision was made to proceed with preparations for getting underway. The weather was expected to calm down later in the day.

"The churning water was too rough for our boat to pull alongside the gangplank to pick the three of us up and transport us to the *Tachin*. So it was decided that we should walk out on the ship's boom and climb down to our boat.

"The distance from the boom to the boat varied from 5 feet to 12 feet as the boat was rocking continually up and down and in and out. It was quite difficult to determine the exact moment to drop into the boat. Thoughts of not surviving the maneuver entered our minds, but somehow we all descended safely and made the trip to the *Tachin.*

"Once on the ship we followed the *Manatee* out to sea and spent the morning getting acquainted with the foreign sailors and their ship. But, because the weather continued to be a problem, it was decided that firing practice would be delayed until the next day.

"The crew was courteous, but only a few could speak English. We had a delicious evening meal—seafood of some kind—better that I didn't know what it was. We were then treated to an American movie that was shown in the mess hall and then shown in our sleeping area in the ship's sick bay.

"The next morning, the weather not improved, word came that the firing practice was to be cancelled altogether. We were to return to the *Manatee* by highline—not at all something you would look forward to. For one thing the water was still turbulent, and for another, the two ships were having difficulty in maintaining the proper distance. A collision at sea, of course, was possible.

"Regardless of the consequences, the lines were stretched across to both ships and a chair was attached to one line. I guess to see if everything worked OK, I was told to go first. I would have just as soon waited—like maybe tomorrow. No luck. I was strapped into the chair and my fellow seamen, my life in their hands, began pulling the cable that would take the chair across the raging sea. At least that was the idea.

"But time and again I sank down near the raging sea and was sprayed with the constantly churning waters. After what seemed like an eternity, I was safely aboard the *Manatee* once more. Then, considering it safe enough, my two companions soon followed."

*　　　*　　　*

Storekeeper William C. Bergmeister said because there was a shooting war still going on, he remembered how dangerous those times were.

"In early July of 1953 there was lots of heavy shelling and one destroyer was low on five-inch ammo, so we high lined several full ammo pallets to that ship. One load took an unfortunate bounce and several five-inch projectiles landed on our port after well deck. Needless to say, there was more than a little concern. But quick-acting deck crew members immediately tossed the shells overboard without further incident.

"Bergmeister said a similar incident happened with the transfer of a 100-pound oxygen tank. It fell to the well deck, he said, damaging its valve and caromed around the well deck until its pressure was lost.

"For me, though, the scariest incident was during one very long tour of duty, two days without sleep, when I was waiting to measure aviation gasoline pumped to an aircraft carrier," he said. "I volunteered to relieve a man assigned to a station-to-station portable head phone. The carrier was ordered on a strike mission and began to pull away, simply letting the four-inch hose dangle from our boom.

"The phone line hung up someplace on the carrier. As it pulled away, it began to pull me. With tension on the line, I was unable to pull free of the phone. As I approached the port lifeline, two hands came from behind me and Ensign Potter was able to release the phone. Into the Sea of Japan it went. And I was saved from a dunking. Thank you, Ensign Potter!"

Bergmeister said that his situation wasn't the only mishap that year. He said that sometime during the winter the ship was refueling a Thai (Siam) destroyer escort off the Korean east coast. The Thai ship was on the Manatee's starboard side and the seas were fairly rough. It was during this time that one of the Thai crewmen fell from their 01 deck to the main deck, landing on his head. They had no medical personnel, so the *Manatee* high lined Hospitalman Third Class Montgomery to assist the injured man.

*   *   *

Most accidents weren't laughing matters, but one accident certainly met all the requirements and had the *Manatee* crew in stitches. Bergmeister explained it this way. "It was in the spring of 1953, and we were off the coast of Korea with a U.S. destroyer on our port side. American destroyers of this vintage were refueled with a four-inch hose using about 100 pounds of pressure. Rather than securing the hose with a flange, the hose was placed down a larger fuel trunk and tied down with heavy lines. On this occasion the hose came loose. black oil (NSFO) proceeded to gush over the bridge and all officers present. It was a funny sight from a distance."

*   *   *

There are accidents of this type and there are accidents that defy definition. Bergmeister said the best example he has of this occurred in the early spring of 1953 while the *Manatee* was on Formosa Straits patrol. Because of the long time period aboard ship the crew was given some free time on Bokoko, an island of the Pescadores group.

"Some of the *Manatee's* crew had built small gasoline powered airplanes," Bergmeister said. "These were controlled by handheld wires. A contingent of Nationalist Chinese soldiers were stationed on the island. They came over to watch. But as the planes were being flown in a circle, the soldiers continued to crowd into the flight pattern of one of the planes. Repeated warnings to stay back weren't heeded. And, as might be expected, one plane had engine problems and came down in a crash landing—right into one of the soldiers."

Bergmeister said that even though the *Manatee* crew gave medical assistance and World War III was averted, the Nationalist Chinese soldier wasn't a happy camper.

*   *   *

"Another unhappy camper was a *Manatee* lookout (his name long faded from memory) who stood watch in the ship's flying bridge during a Condition III in October of 1953." Bergmeister said the lookout's orders included reporting any boats or ships sighted. "So, in due time the lookout called in a sighting of a small fishing boat on the horizon. It wasn't long, however, before the sighting came into full view of the *Manatee* crew.

67

'Correct that,' the lookout started to say. But it was too late. The damage was done. That small fishing boat turned out to be one of the Navy's largest—the battleship USS *Missouri* (BB-63)."

Many things happened in 1953, but the big news that year was the ending of the Korean War. For it was on July 27, 1953, when hostilities ended in the region. On that day an armistice between the United Nations and communist negotiators was signed at Panmunjom, South Korea.

*   *   *

Did Anyone Ask About The Chow?

Two hundred years ago a Sailor might have good reason to complain about the food. Meals served aboard ship often were rancid, consisting of moldy bread topped with whatever was lying around. An American Revolutionary Sailor was served a hard biscuit often infested with weevils, a portion of salt pork, some dried peas and water that was discolored. There were no preservatives other than salt and brine. Food was usually bland and somewhat unpalatable. Only occasionally were there potatoes or turnips.

As the mid 20th century approached, food preservation improved. This allowed a much appreciated broader menu to be offered including many fresh fruits, vegetables and meats. For the most part Manatee Sailors have had good things to say about the food and the ship's cooks who served up the meals. A typical dinner meal might consist of roast beef, mashed potatoes and gravy, green peas, a salad and a piece of apple pie.

CHAPTER 8

1954 FRONT PAGE NEWS

In February and March of 1954 the *Manatee* was part of front page news stories of the day when the ship participated in fleet operations in the Marshall Islands for the first hydrogen bomb tests at Eniwetok Atoll.

Bergmeister said he remembers that time well. "The day before the bomb test we saw the tiny islet and equipment tower where the blast would come from," he said. "But at six in the morning on test day all we felt was a fairly severe roll, even though the 15-megaton bomb delivered a force far more powerful than was expected."

Scientists later said the hydrogen bomb was several times more powerful than the atomic bomb that destroyed Hiroshima, so violent, in fact, that it overwhelmed the measuring instruments and totally vaporized one of the atolls.

Observers said the gigantic mushroom cloud spread at least 100 miles wide. Because the blast had been far greater than expected, some 264 people were exposed to the radiation. This included the crew of a Japanese fishing boat that was within 80 miles of the blast.

The original natives were granted $325,000 in compensation and returned to Bikini in 1974, but four years later they were evacuated once again when new tests showed high levels of residual radioactivity in the region.

Bergmeister said that after the tests *Manatee* headed to Hawaii, but stopped off at Midway Island to supply them with fuel. "Here, while at anchor, the crew could fish," he said. "But no bait was needed, just a hook in the water. Literally hundreds of fish were caught in one day. Some fish the sharks got before being landed. In other cases, gooney birds (albatross) grabbed the fish as they were being pulled from the water.

"Kwajalein and Eniwetok were also island ports of call. It was quite warm here and when we went ashore many of us went for a cool ocean swim. Some had swim trunks others did not. Shortly after entering the water, one or two jeep loads of U.S. Marine MPs arrived, threatening to arrest us for unauthorized swimming. Mainly the problem was we were in the water precisely at the sharks feeding time. Both the sharks and MPs allowed us to go free and unbitten.

"Most of us had only a few beers ashore and we arrived back aboard in reasonable condition. Others, however, had many beers—I mean a lot. And for them it was a different story. It was, in fact, a scene out of the novel, *South Pacific.* Just to get them aboard, wire stretchers were used instead of the usual cargo nets. Then several white jumpers were torn off when these men were too drunk to undress themselves. The Naval Commanding Officer ashore sent a message to *Manatee* ordering our crew not to come back ashore.

When the ship finally entered Pearl Harbor in Hawaii, the ship was once again in the middle of a landmark news-making event—well, sort of. Bergmeister said that on April 1, 1954, the PA system on the ship was playing music and news from a local radio station. Suddenly there was a flash announcement. A newscaster stated that the Territory of Hawaii had just been admitted to the union as a state, and as a welcoming gesture, income tax for 1954 would be forgiven for the islanders.

This, of course, was great news, and not just because of the tax benefit, but because the citizens of Hawaii had, in fact, already ratified a proposed constitution and had been expecting action. But as historians will tell you, Congress didn't get around to passing a Hawaii statehood bill until 1959, followed by President Eisenhower signing the bill on March 18. Then the statehood wasn't to be official until Aug. 21, 1959. Needless to say the radio broadcast was a little premature, all part of an April Fools' Day prank.

On Oct. 22, 1954, Captain Joseph S. Lewis relieved Commander F. A. Brock as commanding officer. A few days later the ship entered Craig shipyard in Long Beach for repairs and maintenance.

*   *   *

CHAPTER 9

1955-1956 NOW, HOW ABOUT SOME OF THAT HIGH SCHOOL SPIRIT?

When most of us entered the Navy we were fresh out of high school, still familiar with those special colors, mascots and sports teams. Few of us had not lost that good ole school spirit, at least not right away. But the question was—could some of this enthusiasm be transferred to those of us serving aboard the *Manatee*?

Let's see, what do you think? With the draft in full force, rather than the Army getting us we joined the Navy. That was good... well, maybe. We gave up those school football, baseball and basketball games. We gave up school dances. We gave up going to the drive-in with that someone special. The give-up list, as I remember, did get rather long.

What we got in place of this was endless days of chipping paint, swabbing decks, standing watch at wee hours of the night... you know the rest. And, speaking of rest, we found that on the *Manatee* there just wasn't all that much of it.

That summer, in the midst of those long months of re-fueling operations in the Western Pacific, an idea was brewing. The *Manatee's* "cheering-up-the-crew" officer devised a slogan—"Qu Superavit!" which supposedly meant, "Who Shall Excel Her," probably in Swahili or some other little-used language.

A ship's flag was devised using this slogan and an emblem of a sea cow was created. And you could bet (but don't bet much just yet) that the men on the *Manatee* were excited. They just couldn't wait to show off their wares. They didn't have to wait long. It was time now for *Manatee* to replenish the ships in Task Force 77.

As the first ship came alongside—the *Manatee* flag went up the pole. Then there was that second ship. The flag went up again. That ship left and a third ship came alongside. It seems nobody on the other ships noticed. Or, if they did, they just didn't care. What these Sailors on the other ships did care about, it seems, was to get this refueling business over with so that they could go back to their naps.

The result of all of this is that the "good ole school spirit" idea redirected to those serving on the *Manatee* may not have worked. But it didn't matter now. News spread that the ship had completed its Western Pacific duty and was to be heading home. Now, there was joy in Mudville.

The *Manatee* had been away from the states since Feb. 23 and was now returning in late September. A month later it was out to sea once again, but just for a short trip up the coast to San Francisco Bay. Included in some needed repairs was the installation of new messing and berthing facilities which made life aboard the ship a little more comfortable. It was here that Captain J. S. Lewis was detached and Captain William Blenman took command.

*   *   *

By January 1956, the *Manatee* was ready once again for some extended days at sea. First it was just a trip down the coast to Long Beach and San Diego. Then, on March 23, it was back to Japan, arriving in Yokosuka on August 8. A month later the *Manatee* was in the Philippines, then on to Formosa and back to Japan before a well-looked-forward-to five-day stay in Hong Kong, where the crew traditionally took advantage of the great buys and stocked up on gifts and personal goods to take home.

By the end of September the ship would be back in Long Beach and San Diego where Captain Blenman bid the ship goodbye and Captain R. L. Neyman took command.

*   *   *

A Few
Good
Men

Plus

Two

More

LEFT: BM 3rd Class George W. Smith, Jr. was assigned to the Manatee from 1944 to 1946.
BELOW: 3rd Class Yeoman Theron Gailey taking a break before those "no-smoking-in indoor-work-area" days.

FACING PAGE:

FAR LEFT TOP: Royce Godwin who was on board during World War II.
FAR LEFT BOTTOM: John Werner who served from 1971 to 1973.
TOP LEFT: Dan Mehner who served from 1952 to 1955.
TOP RIGHT: Sam Hartley
LEFT: Farroll Barrett gets some recognition for his good work.

CHAPTER 10

1957 WHERE-OH-WHERE DID THE *MANATEE* GO?

Fortunately, it doesn't happen very often. But this did happen to eleven *Manatee* Sailors who were on liberty while the ship was ported in Japan in 1957. They did all the right things. They got their liberty passes, put together only what they needed for the day, checked the time they needed to be back, and like all good *Manatee* Sailors, quick as a flash they were gone for new adventures off the ship.

But what these eleven Sailors didn't realize was that they would be gone for quite a bit longer than they had expected. With liberty nearly up they arrived back at the pier only to discover the ship wasn't there. They re-checked their liberty passes. No problem there, they were OK. They re-checked the number marked on the pier. No problem there. There was, however, a problem. There was no ship.

It seems that while the eleven Sailors were out having a good time, the ship got an urgent call to leave port immediately and join a task force that needed fuel and needed it right then. "But... but... but... we have Sailors ashore," must have been the message in return. "No buts—just leave and leave right now"—had to have been the answer.

Fortunately most of the crew had already arrived back on board the ship, but the ship couldn't wait the two more hours or so before liberty was up. So, just shy of 8 p.m. the ship set sail for lands unknown. The Sailors who had arrived at the dock, with time to spare, had no choice but to report to shore facilities, contact the ship and find out "what now?"

The "what now" turned out to be, "hang in there." Eventually the USS *Regulus* (AF-57) picked up all eleven men. Five days later, on June 13, they were high-lined from the *Regulus* to the *Mana-*

76

tee. And, for those eleven men, an adventurous extended liberty was over.

*   *   *

Now, with all that fun behind them, the *Manatee* crew was now in the midst of some of its worst sea duty. The crew replenished the carriers *Yorktown* (CV-12), *Philippine Sea* (CV-47), and *Lexington* (CV-16) as well as the cruisers *Columbus* (CA-74) and *Helena* (CA-75), the last of which was the flag ship carrying the admiral in charge of the 7th Fleet.

The weather at this time couldn't have been worse. During replenishment from both sides of the *Manatee* simultaneously, several men were injured by heavy seas crashing over the well deck. It happened to be a week of almost continuous replenishments of about 25 ships ranging from carriers to destroyer escorts.

Following this, there was a brief return to Sasebo, Japan, but only to go back to sea two days later. This time it was to replenish 12 destroyers, two carriers and a cruiser. And if the *Manatee* crew thought the weather was bad before, it was even worse this time around. Darkness plus 15-foot waves caused several hoses to part and made station keeping almost impossible. If the men thought it couldn't get any worse—they were wrong. Because now with the storm over, for long periods of time there was another situation: dense fog. Hardly anyone could see what they were doing.

Fortunately, none of this bad weather lasted. And once again there were good times ahead. That included ample days of liberty in various ports. Then, even in all the replenishment assignments that followed, the conditions were favorable the entire time.

*   *   *

Should a Navy ship have an open house, and it does so occasionally, the first place most visitors want to go is the bridge. That's where those large steering wheels are located which are often as big as or bigger than the person doing the steering. Today's ships are run electronically and making those turns and staying on course are not an issue. You just plug all the information into a computer and you're ready to go. You don't even have those large helms. These wheels, or helms as they are called, were standard issue on ships going back to the beginning of those ocean-going sailing vessels. And they were used on those large ships right into the 20th century, the *Manatee*'s entire sea-going career being no exception.

Shipmates standing watch had their turn at the helm, making sure the ship stayed on course. For the most part it wasn't all that complicated. You just kept your eye on the established compass setting. If the ship drifted a little in one direction you just turned the wheel a little, moving it back on course.

Such was the case when Chuck Rains, who later became a Gunners Mate Third Class Petty Officer, was on his first voyage on the *Manatee* and just learning the helm. "We were just approaching Japan," he said. "It was very hot and humid early that morning and the ship was rocking from the swells. Everything in the pilot house was wet from the humidity and sea spray, including the tile floors."

Rains said that there were a lot of small fishing boats in the area and the executive officer was moving from one side of the bridge to the other watching out for these fishing boats. "I was standing in front of the helm watching the helmsman who was teaching me the process. It had been a long period of time, since four that morning, and I was tired as I had been standing there almost the entire four-hour watch.

"Then, as I was shifting my feet, the executive officer was running by and I accidently tripped him. He fell flat on the deck and his momentum made him slide on the wet deck all the way across the pilot house. When he got up the front of his uniform was completely wet. I could see that he wasn't all that happy. Needless to say, I stayed out of his way after that."

*   *   *

Rains said that sometimes, just as you get the hang of things, the Navy inserts something new, expecting you to know how to handle things. "Once I was standing a helm watch as I did every day we were at sea and we had a rendezvous with other ships in the South China Sea. It was a convoy exercise where we all steered a sinuous course for a period of minutes and then steered a common heading together. I had never been involved in such a course exercise before and had no training in it. Then out of the blue, the officer of the deck approached me and turned on the sweeping needle on the compass card. He then told me to keep our heading on the needle as it swept back and forth. This made the ship follow the sinuous course. If this sounds complicated, well, it was.

"I also didn't know, of course, that this was a timed exercise where we would steer the sinuous course for a period of time and then stop following the needle and steer straight ahead for some minutes. Then it would be back to the sinuous course again.

"When the officer of the deck said secure from the sinuous steering I thought we were finished and I turned the needle off as it was a distraction. Bad move. A few minutes later the officer said to prepare to go to the sinuous steering again. So, I turned the needle back on again, not realizing I should not have turned it off to begin with.

"As it happened, when I turned the needle on again, it was 180 degrees out of phase as the needles on the other ships in the convoy. When the officer gave me the mark to start following the needle again I was turning toward the ships alongside us in the convoy. It is difficult to see around the helm. The first indication that I had screwed up was a frantic voice over the loudspeaker from our sister ship—'You're cutting across our bow.'

"Immediately the officer of the deck hollered 'right full rudder' which I immediately did and we avoided a collision. The officer gave me a long hard look, but didn't say anything to me. He radioed the other ships and said we had a malfunction on our compass card. Needless to say, I was relieved from the helm for the rest of the exercise. But from those daily helm watches? No such luck."

*   *   *

By November, the *Manatee* was back to the states and on December 19, 1957 Captain H. P. Holmshaw relieved Captain Neyman as commanding officer in an impressive ceremony at Long Beach.

Here's What You Could Buy With Those Navy Salaries.

If you were a Third Class Petty Officer (E-4) in the Navy in 1949-1950, you were making $117.60 per month. In those years it would cost you 10 cents for a bottle of Coke, 18 cents for a gallon of gas, 12 cents for a loaf of bread and $1,420 for a new car.

By 1952-1962 pay was raised to $122.30 at which time you had to pay 24 cents for a gallon of gas, four cents for a postage stamp, and $88 for an airplane ticket from Los Angeles to New York. A new house would set you back $2,390.

Pay was raised in 1965 to $165. A letter would cost you five cents to mail and gas was up to 31 cents. McDonalds was selling their hamburgers for 20 cents, a real bargain then.

Just two years later, in 1967, the pay was again raised to $177.90. A new car then would cost you $2,822, rent $130, bread 22 cents and a movie ticket $1.50.

The Manatee was decommissioned in 1973 and these Sailors were making $369.90. This may have been due to the Vietnam War. Expenses were rising as well. Gas was now 38 cents a gallon and sending a letter cost nine cents

Today (2016) pay stands at $2,046 per month.

CHAPTER 11

1958-1959 RESPONDING TO
A CRISIS IN FORMOSA

In 1958 the ship was scheduled for only four months deployment in the Western Pacific. This was from mid-May through mid-September. But, as with most well-laid plans, things happened. There was another crisis. This time there were problems in Formosa over the Quemoy and Matsu Islands.

The turmoil turned into a shooting match on August 23, 1959. It was then that communist Chinese artillery batteries began shelling National Chinese forces on the offshore islands of Matsu and Quemoy. This prompted President Dwight D. Eisenhower to dispatch elements of the 7th Fleet, which included the *Manatee*, to support and transport supplies from Formosa to Nationalist troops on Quemoy. The force, which included six aircraft carriers, was a show of resolve and it was enough to end the crisis by December. Because of this, the *Manatee* extended its stay another month to service the ships called to the area to help quell the problem.

Now, safely back in the states and after the crew was given some well-earned leave, the *Manatee* once again changed commanding officers. Captain Holmshaw was relieved by Captain John J. Lynch, a naval aviator who had just recently completed a tour of duty as naval attaché in Moscow, Russia.

Captain Lynch only had a few weeks to get acquainted with the crew before the *Manatee*, on March 24, was off once again to the Western Pacific. The ship stopped off in Hawaii, but this time only for 12 hours, before it steamed on to Sasebo, Japan, which had over the years become its home port in the Western Pacific.

*   *   *

On May 28, during replenishment with the aircraft carrier USS *Hornet* (CV-12) and her escorts, eight men on the *Manatee* were injured when large waves broke across the forward tank deck. If that wasn't bad enough, there was this. But first, some background.

While refueling, most often with a ship on each side, all vessels are required to maintain the exact speed and the exact distance from each other. But one day, as *Manatee* Sailor Leroy Andrews remembers, "The aircraft carrier, USS *Hornet* lost control of its steering while hooked up to a refueling hose. Needless to say the hose broke and oil splattered big time over our ship as well as over several of our crew," Andrews said.

"Regardless, the carrier still needed fuel. So the decision was made that we would clean the mess up the next day on the *Manatee* while the carrier fixed its steering problem. The next day came and with the steering problem fixed and the *Manatee* cleaned up, we were at it again. This time, however, we saw a line tossed to us. Attached to it was a note saying the carrier's crew had a special gift for us. Then, high-lined across was a very large sheet cake, decorated with a likeness of the *Manatee* on one side, their ship on the other. And in between the two ships was a broken hose and 'oil,' created with chocolate frosting, spurting everywhere. Then, in big frosted letters, on top of the cake were two words—'Sorry fellows.'"

Now, returning to the *Manatee* clean-up the day before, Andrews said it was accomplished in an unexpected way—bribery. "That's right." Andrews said. "The captain said if we get the clean -up done by noon we would have swim call. That's when all who wished could take a dip in the pool, the pool being the Pacific Ocean. The incentive was enough to get the job done with minutes to spare. So, both the liberty and whale boats were launched, each one complete with two armed volunteers to keep watch for sharks.

"At the same time the 'stop main engines' order was given and cargo nets were thrown over the side, this to give the swimmers an easy return up the side of the ship. Then, one by one, we dove off the *Manatee* deck into what was then nice warm water. Once back on board, as usual, we had a silent muster and then with all shipmates accounted for, it was back to work."

*   *   *

Following the *Manatee's* four-month Western Pacific duty in 1959, the ship was chosen to take part in a joint Canadian-American replenishment demonstration. This was held October 8, for the 14th Annual Conference of the National Defense Transportation Association. The demonstration was staged in Puget Sound with six American ships and two Canadian destroyers. Unusual in this was the fact that the ships, which included the *Manatee*, were boarded by more than 1,000 people as observers. And they stayed aboard as the ships got underway and proceeded with the demonstrations.

At the end of October, the *Manatee* had returned to Long Beach where Captain Lynch was relieved of command by another naval aviator, Captain John C. Kelly.

*   *   *

Remembering Those Letters Home

OIL TANKER

UNITED STATES NAVY

U.S.S. Manatee AO-58

A commemorative envelope of Navy oil tankers. This one postmarked with the USS *Manatee* stamp in 1955. Note the three cent postage stamp.

CHAPTER 12

1960 WHEN NO ONE HAD
THE BLUE PLATE SPECIAL

If you think you've heard them all when it comes to old sea stories, then wait until you listen to the tales by *Manatee* Personnel Man Third Class Mack Matesen. His wife and two daughters, he says, are bored silly with them. But it's because he has retold them so many times already, that we get the benefit of the details. And wow—are there details!

Like when the ship was in Guam one Christmas, when the temperature outside was 100 plus. "Mail call came and my mother sent me three pounds of fudge, which she duly packed in between wax paper," he said. "When I popped the lid the fudge had melted into one massive blob. See what hundred degree temperatures will do! Well, two buddies and I snatched a couple of large tablespoons from the mess deck, closed our eyes and chowed down on the brown mass like there was no tomorrow."

Matesen said he later sent a thank you letter home mentioning the melted fudge. She wrote back, saying, "I don't understand. I sent another batch to your older brother. There was no mention of it melting." Matesen said he understood. His brother, who was in the Air Force, was stationed in Iceland.

*   *   *

There was another incident when the ship was at the fueling depot at Buckner Bay in the Philippine Islands. "We had an old gunner's mate, whom we called 'Pappie' because he was a grey-haired, grandfatherly-like guy. But this guy liked his booze. One evening he had a real snoot full and was stupid enough to relieve the duty petty officer at the quarterdeck. He was so drunk he had to hold onto a stanchion.

"The officer on duty was a young 20-something Lieutenant Junior Grade O'Shea who was more than a little concerned about the situation, particularly because Pappie had a side arm and wasn't about to relinquish it. What to do? Things, in fact, got a little tense until an old crusty chief took charge, relieved Pappie of his sidearm and with some help from others, carted him off to his bunk to sleep it off."

*   *   *

And then there was the time when the *Manatee* was in the waters of Quendy and Matsu. "We had a commitment to fuel the USS *Shasta (AE-33)* so it could stay on station and give fire support to the land forces," Matesen said. "It was around dusk, we were at our fueling station and this hard-charging commanding officer on the frigate came out of nowhere, scooting up the port side. But he misjudged his approach and hit us dead on, damaging and jamming our screw."

Matesen said the *Manatee* skipper took the incident well and had a good sense of humor about it, probably because he had this idea of what he would do next. "After the damage was repaired and we got out of dry dock, this captain had a very large (like 20-by-40-foot) band-aid painted on the back of the ship. We had more than our share of questions from ships we fueled thereafter—asking, 'why the...?'"

* * *

Then there was the time that the USS *Black* (DD-666) really earned its name. Seems the *Manatee* was refueling the vessel when the *Black* lost steerage, and as she was pulling away laterally, the span wire at the after pumping station was getting tighter and tighter. Matesen said the captain ordered an immediate shutdown but the span wire started to split before they could even stop pumping. "The second division deck crew saw what was happening and scattered," Matesen said. "No one wanted to be around when that cable lashed back in *Manatee's* direction."

Matesen said that two Sailors on the *Black* used a sledge hammer to bust the holding device, and in doing so, the pumping line ripped out of the tank, completely dousing oil over the two Sailors and completely over the ship's stern to boot. In other words—the *Black* turned black.

* * *

Other memories: "There was the time when the 3rd Class Exams were to take place and the officer who was to administer the exams, Lieutenant Junior Grade O'Shea, was drunk as a skunk. From that day forward the Executive Officer, Lieutenant Commander A. R. Kenworthy called him 'Bird Legs,' one of many names Kenworthy had for various officers aboard the *Manatee*.

Noteworthy also is that it was Kenworthy who hatched up the idea that had the whole *Manatee* crew not wanting their evening meal. Can you believe Sailors not wanting to eat? It had to be something mighty big. Seems that the captain received orders to proceed to the port of Chen Hei, Korea, where the ship would be met in the harbor by a small civilian boat. In it was the body of a retired lieutenant commander who had died. The family, it seemed, wanted him to be buried at sea.

Matesen said that when the body was hoisted aboard, ship's company had a dilemma. What to do with the body for the day or so before it could be dispatched into the sea? At first it was thought it could be tied down on the deck somewhere—but where? Kenworthy's idea, however, was chosen by the captain. The deceased would be stored in the meat locker, that big walk-in freezer just across from the laundry and caddy corner to the barber shop. It was, of course, to be kept secret from the crew.

"Well, Matesen said, "the word leaked out. And as luck would have it, beef stew was on the bill of fare for that evening's meal. First class petty officers, as usual, had first chow call privileges and took the opportunity to tell all that the cooks had dug up a little fresh meat for the stew. You can take it from there. I guarantee you, not a soul aboard had that blue plate special."

On November 23, 1960, it was time for another change. Captain Kelly was relieved of duty by Captain Charles Onea Akers.

*   *   *

TOP: Chinese junk navigates through Hong Kong Harbor. BELOW: A bridge in Japan, not one to drive a truck over, but great for photos. RIGHT: Some families didn't get the word on advancements in transportation. FACING PAGE: Larry McIntosh enjoys both the eats and the service in Tokyo in the summer of 1962.

The Views Are Great And The Eats Exceptional—On The Other Side Of The World

CHAPTER 13

1961 REMEMBERING THOSE
FUN TIMES AT THE PIKE

There is probably no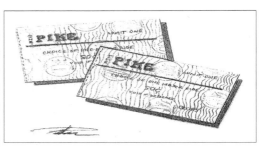
Manatee Sailor who
doesn't remember The
Pike in Long Beach, Cali-
fornia. For throughout the
ship's history from the
1940s into the 1970s the
Pike was "the" place to
go when the ship was home ported in Long Beach. The Pike, of
course, was a street a mile long, solidly lined with amusements of
every kind. It was right on the beach near downtown.

It was a place that if you were blind, you couldn't miss it. For, if
the music didn't do its duty, the noise from the various facilities
and attractions or the barkers with megaphones luring the unsus-
pecting to games of chance would. Among them was a horse race
game, a shooting gallery with, a dart game and a theater. There
was the kiddy fish ride, The Pikes tattoo shop, the Fun House,
bumper cars and the Laughing Lady.

But, most of all, there was the Cyclone Racer which at one time
was the largest and fastest coaster in the United States. It was on
this that the operators claimed there were 17 deaths. There was a
Ferris wheel, a carousel, a Tilt-A-Whirl and a pony ride. There
was an indoor swimming pool called The Plunge and dozens of
fast food shops dishing out hamburgers and hot dogs with all the
trimmings.

If that wasn't enough, there was the Rainbow Ballroom and Bar,
the Hollywood on The Pike Show Bar, the Spit and Argue Club
and the Glue Pot Bar. In fact, there were honky-tonk beer parlors
of every type, particularly on the east end of the walk.

90

But among the most interesting spots was a Believe It Or Not-type side show which, among its features, was what many thought was a dummy made of fiberglass and leather. What it was, in fact, was the mortal remains of Ken McGrath who was a mummified bank robber that was killed by a posse near Guthrie, Oklahoma, on October 7, 1911.

It seems that when no one claimed the body, the undertaker stuck it in a corner of his shop where it stayed for five years. That was until a traveling side show came into possession of the embalmed remains and exhibited him as "The Famous Oklahoma Outlaw." Later, the body was sold to a carnival which made its way around the United States for many years. Somehow it ended up at The Pike. Over the years no one believed it was real. But when the shop went out of business and the "dummy" was being moved someone not only discovered the body to be something more than fiberglass and leather, but identified it as the actual remains of a person, the outlaw Ken McGrath.

So, 66 years after his death, McGrath was shipped back to Guthrie, Oklahoma, and was buried in the Summit View Cemetery, right next to another outlaw, Bill Doolin.

*   *   *

It was at The Pike that Shirley, better known as Big Red, worked. She said she started her employment the same day that Gunners Mate Second Class Carlie (Shorty) Miracle reported aboard the *Manatee* in February of 1961. And it wasn't long before Big Red would soon be given another name— Shirley (Big Red) Miracle.

"At this time the *Manatee* was a party ship," Shirley said. "The crew worked hard, but played harder. And although there were at least 20 bars on The Pike, The Hollywood on the Pike, where I worked, was a real favorite. For not only did it have live entertainment, but there were bells, whistles and air hoses in the floor to blow skirts up," she said.

"I worked days there for a year, and the men of the *Manatee* had to be the most inventive of any ship. But whatever they did, it was always in good fun. I remember, for instance, as an unofficial member of the crew, that I stood shore patrol in the Pier E parking lot, complete with whistle, arm band and Peacoat."

Shirley continued, "I remember bringing unauthorized 'refreshments' aboard the *Manatee*. They were strapped around my waist with a belt and over this was a very large coat. I rattled all the way up the gang plank."

Manatee crew members, she said, enjoyed leap-frogging over the Pike's large cement elephant trash cans. And when riled, one *Manatee* Sailor, who was African-American, often stated that he didn't think it was right that Indians had all the fun scalping their enemies. It was believed that if he was ever elected president he probably would change things.

The Miracles were married just six days before the *Manatee* left on a nine-plus months cruise, well over 40 years ago. And for all those years the marriage stayed intact. But, what didn't was the Pike. Everything came to an end there in 1979. It would be six years after the *Manatee* would meet its demise in a scrap yard. The town of Long Beach also moved on to other things, as did the former *Manatee* Sailors.

*　　*　　*

But now we're getting ahead of ourselves. It is still 1961 and the good and bad memories of duty on the *Manatee* just don't end that easily. Mack Matesen, for instance, still remembers those times when rough seas made just getting into the chow line an adventure.

"If you want to put a name on it, you can call it a 'sprint to eat,' the chore of getting from point A to point B without going overboard," Matesen said. "When the old bucket was loaded with fuel, the well deck to the water line looked like no more than around four or five feet. Underway in a storm we'd take water over the sides in giant green waves.

"I'd come up the ladder, there on the starboard side, un-dog the hatch and step out into a real adventure. You'd have to time it just right before another wave would crash over those long wooden planks above the well deck. And then you would have to run like hell for the stern area. Then you'd cross over to the port side to try to be protected by the aft part of the ship as you scooted along the deck and into the galley area."

*　　*　　*

Tensions between the U.S. and the Soviet Union were on edge at this time. And U.S.-Cuba relations were heating up with the Bay of Pigs invasion. There was also unrest in several Asian nations with the rapid expansion of communism. So it was in this period of time that Fred Loveland recalled an alert while several ships were docked in Subic Bay, the Philippines.

"I remember being on liberty when the MPs came around and ordered all U.S. Naval personnel back to their ships," Loveland said. "The shouts I heard were, 'We're going to war boys.' And even though the crew was aboard and all the other ships had disappeared to parts unknown, the *Manatee* was in the process of repairing a boiler and it couldn't go anywhere. So the ship remained for another couple of days before it could join the fleet. Fortunately no shots were fired at that time and there was no war. But the alert certainly woke everyone up to that possibility."

*　　*　　*

While all of this was going on with the *Manatee*, I (Joe Kraus) was safely back home in Portland, Oregon, and made the mistake of opening up a letter. I was to report for a physical. That was the bad news. The good news, I guess, was that the physical was to be paid for by someone else. But then more bad news: The payee was going to be the United States Army.

I went, but surely, I thought, they would find something wrong so the Army wouldn't want me and I could go back to enjoying

93

the good life as an over-the-hill teenager. Sure enough, they found something. They put before my eyes some large cards with some dots on them. Then they asked me to read the numbers in the middle of the dots. What dots? What numbers?

Sure enough—I had a bad case, a very bad case of color blindness. Throughout my life nobody told me that those trees on the hillside were green, not gray. Then there was this thing about all those white cars I was seeing. Turns out they were light green.

"So, I guess I won't be drafted?" I asked.

"Well, let's see," the medical guy said as he put his hand to his chin. "Because of your eye problem, they won't want you in a submarine." He explained that each of those colored lights on an operations board meant something. If I pushed the wrong one, the sub might pop up rather quickly or go down to the bottom, possibly even bump into a whale. But worse, I might launch a bunch of torpedoes at some Girl Scouts in a canoe."

"Thank goodness," I said. "Then I can go home and relax?"

"You can do that, but only for about two weeks. It's then when you'll get this letter from the Army," he said. "You see, the Army doesn't care what color you see when you strap on that 100-pound backpack, walk uphill 50 miles, dig a foxhole, then, desperately hungry, you open and eat a can of cold C-rations."

Needless to say, within two days I had visited a U.S. Navy recruiting office and signed up for duty. They would be happy, they said, to let the Army know that now I was beyond their jurisdiction. I guess I was happy as well…well, maybe a little bit.

Meanwhile, on the *Manatee*, it was time for another switch. Captain Akers, who was aboard just one year, was relieved of duty by Captain Herman Trum III who would, much later, become a rear admiral.

CHAPTER 14

1962 THE *MANATEE* HOSTS
ITS FIRST STOW-A-WAY

Coming aboard the *Manatee* in the first part of 1962 was Robert Musgrave, just out of "A" school, who would be assigned to the engine room. It was Musgrave, in fact, who blew the whistle on what was at that time a deeply-held secret. Musgrave did wait until the ruckus was over, causing no harm to those involved. It all concerned another *Manatee* Sailor, Ralph McWhirter and what was to become a genuine stow-a-way.

"It all started at Knott's Berry Farm in Southern California," Musgrave said. "McWhirter enjoyed his stay at the entertainment complex so much that he decided to take back with him a souvenir. In this case it was a live one—a chicken.

McWhirter may have reasoned that the chicken would enjoy life aboard ship and the Sailors would either enjoy the female company, or if nothing else, some fresh eggs. Whatever, the hen found a home in the ship's engine room and was fed every day with the finest feed the ship's mess hall could provide, crewmembers in turn providing all the necessities.

The caper only lasted undetected for about a week, when the officer in charge discovered the unauthorized ship's company. Its fate was held in the balance until the ship made its first port of call at Pearl Harbor. And soon after, as luck would have it, the chicken found a new home with a Hawaiian family.

*   *   *

Musgrave said McWhirter wasn't the only unusual person aboard the ship at that time. "I remember one shipmate, Seaman Walker," Musgrave said. "It didn't fail—every time we needed him he wasn't there. For hours at a time we had no idea where he was. And this went on not just for one day, but for several days, until, of course, the work day was over. That's when he would appear as if nothing was amiss. Walker just didn't want to put up with the hassle he was getting. So, should someone ask where he had been, he would have several excuses at the ready as an answer. He was his own missing persons bureau."

*   *   *

For Musgrave, however, he had his own problems. One of them was his favorite off-duty experiences. And top on this list was attending the local bars that were designated 'off limits' to servicemen. His favorite of these was The Black Rose in Sasebo, Japan, which, he said, regularly got tore up in Sailor brawls.

Several *Manatee* Sailors, in fact, remembered that The Black Rose, and other 'off-limits' drinking establishments like it, were popular with Sailors willing to take the chance that they wouldn't get caught. The bars, in turn, expected trouble and prepared for it by trying as much as possible to protect their equipment and supplies. They said that in Australia, for instance, drinking by the natives in those days was a national duty. Some of the bars there would even play patriotic music just to rile up those customers of a different nationality. Why they provoked fights in their establishments, was another question. Some thought it was because this is what made their particular bar so popular.

*   *   *

For me (Joe Kraus), the "happiness" of civilian life got a little bit dulled at the beginning of 1962. Following boot camp, with orders in hand, I stood on a Long Beach, California, pier and looked up to the ship before me —the USS *Manatee*. I, of course, expected a sleek-looking cruiser complete with the big guns or, better yet, an aircraft carrier with a fancy name like the *Enterprise* or the *Hornet*. Instead, this ship was not sleek nor was it necessarily good looking. Well, let's faces it - the *Manatee* was a floating gas station. What would I tell my friends back home?

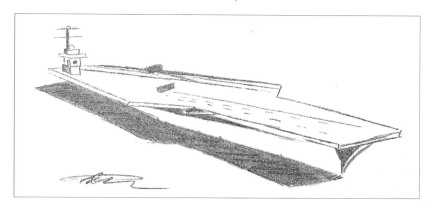

I was first assigned to first division which turned out to be a group of talented scrapers, painters, scrubbers, and mop and bucket specialists. It was the kind of work you did when you got into trouble, growing up as a kid. So I learned rather quickly that my boss at that time—Third Class Boatswain's Mate Curtis Betts was the one to avoid as much as possible, otherwise, he'd find something for me to do. And it usually wasn't pleasant.

For me, those inefficiencies in joyful living lasted only a few months. During that time I quickly earned a seaman's rank and hit the books to become a yeoman. I made it on May 16, 1962, and was made a third class petty officer. I thought that maybe this would put me on another ship. It didn't. I was quickly assigned to the *Manatee*'s own ship's office. There, I did the standard office duties and kept the ship's log. On my own I also founded a ship's newspaper I called *The Sea Scoop*, keeping the crew up on the news of the day during those long periods at sea.

But, whatever misgivings I had when I first reported aboard the ship, eventually vanished. For, within 24 hours, the ship left the pier heading for the high seas, first to Hawaii and for me the ultimate adventure—a visit to ports in the Pacific Ocean and Asia. It would be my first experience aboard a ship and my first, with the exception of British Columbia Canada, visit to another country.

*   *   *

My baptism by fire came some weeks later when we pulled into Subic Bay in the Philippines. And here, after what seemed to be an eternity aboard ship, we were set loose on liberty. One full day it was to do whatever I wished. And that was in a country I knew little about. Only, in fact, what I learned in my geography class in high school. And, because time was limited, all of us had to stay pretty much in the city of Olongapo.

Due to a severe rainy season at that time, the roads out of town, I was told, were often impassable. Even in the best of weather buses had to contend with roads that were mountainous, dusty or muddy. Keeping a standardized bus schedule was out of the question. And arrival times, if you arrived at all, were certainly not guaranteed.

My disadvantage was that I would be entirely on my own. All my shipmates that I knew well at that time had only one destination in mind. And that was to the nearest bar. As a non-drinker, that wasn't my idea of a good time. No, I wanted to explore. And that I did.

The first thing I noticed, however, was the never-ending line of bars—one after another on Rizal Avenue and Magsaysay Street on what seemed to be Olongapo's only thoroughfare. Mixed in were cheap hotels and massage parlors. Outside each were folks enticing all who walked by to come in and sample the merchandise. Everywhere there were those folks of all ages trying to sell their trinkets and ready-to-eat food that did not in the least look appetizing. I would later be told that most of this was monkey meat on a stick. If this wasn't already a cultural shock, there was one more—being offered a commodity not on view—their sisters.

All of these things, of course, were geared to separate us from our meager supply of money. Many Sailors left behind their supposedly born-and-bred civilized behavior, behavior they acquired back in their home town or on the ship, only to be reactivated once again on their return.

Missing in Olongapo were the clean streets, the sidewalks, the variety of stores and shops— all organized in the community where I came from, Portland, Oregon. Missing also were the smells of rose gardens, evergreen trees and green grass in the parks. In their place was a sort-of musty smell, the aroma of rotting eggs, the stench of an open sewer. Only later did I find out that the town had the reputation of being the dirtiest, most degenerate port in all our travels in the Western Pacific.

On the outskirts of town, what you saw were bamboo huts built on stilts over a dirty, brownish river bed. This, I was told, was the fetid Po River (also called the Bajac River). And even worse was the scene of dozens of young kids swimming away, no worries of what diseases awaited them. In some parts of the river Sailors would throw coins and watch the kids dive for each one, compounding the problem.

We were warned to watch our wallets wherever we went and that certain parts of town that were off-limits. Once I was off the ship, those boundary lines got a little blurred. If it looked safe and there were so warning signs—there I went.

If I got tired of walking, I would ride on what seemed to be the only mode of transportation—jeepneys.

What enterprising local residents did was to take those old leftover World War II U.S. Army jeeps, decorate them in flowery colors and run them in a steady stream along Rizal Avenue. You hopped aboard one and rode it until it reached an area that looked interesting. And then you hopped off. After that, it was on again and off again other jeepneys, until you had no other place to go.

The Olongapo we knew in those early days, however, is no more. It rose from a "sin city" in the 1960s and 1970s to become a model city of nearly 250,000. The Navy has moved out, the bars, cheap hotels and other establishments have closed down. What has not ended are the memories.

*   *   *

After those few days of liberty we were all back aboard the ship and now it was off to Japan. Before our arrival, however, I met a shipmate who had similar interests as I did in taking advantage of sightseeing and travel in each port of call. And like me, he was not interested in visiting the bars. Meet W. S. Akyiama, a Sailor who reported aboard the *Manatee* shortly after I did that same year. He was from Honolulu, Hawaii, and was of Japanese ancestry. But, best of all, was the fact he didn't drink, he wanted to sightsee and he spoke some Japanese.

So our liberty days consisted of going down to the nearest train station and heading out as far as we could to see as much country as possible. It wasn't long before our two-some expanded to three, four and sometimes as many as eight of us—all on journeys of exploration. Akyiama, of course, continued his duties as our official interpreter.

These journeys took us to museums, national parks, historical sites and farming areas where we watched, here in the early 1960s, farming done by hand and animal-drawn carts and hauling of material with long poles over their shoulders. We found out later that these poles held buckets of human-originated fertilizer. Just glad we didn't offer to help.

We went to a baseball game where we, in our Sailor uniforms, turned out to be one of the attractions. We went to plays and concerts and watched fishermen haul in their catches for the day. Everywhere we were greeted respectfully, some residents wanting to practice their English, others reaching out for handshakes.

Only once did we feel totally unwelcome and that was at the Hiroshima Atomic Bomb Museum. Here, overlooking the ruined World War II dome, the only remnant of that blast, we were at the epicenter of that wartime event that led to the end of that terrible war. Looking at the exhibits, in our U.S. Navy uniforms, was uncomfortable for us as it must have been for the Japanese visitors.

During these excursions, my most embarrassing moment came when I was in a train station and had to go to the restroom. When a news vender pointed out where it was, I went in and proceeded in doing my duty when a group of young schoolgirls walked in and passed by directly behind me as if nothing was amiss. I panicked, thinking I had gone into the women's room by mistake. I hadn't. This, like many other restrooms in Japan at the time, was co-ed.

*   *   *

Back on the *Manatee*, I remember Sundays as a day of rest. Work consisted of only that which was absolutely necessary in addition to the regular four-hour watches. It was rare, but sometimes if we crossed the International Date Line just right, we got two Sundays in one week. What a kick!

When we were out to sea there was no opportunity to go to church. But I remember this young black Sailor who was on board at the time who had a great personality. I don't remember his name, but I do remember that he talked a few of us into creating an on-board non-denominational Sunday service. We prepared a few short talks, picked out a few songs and assigned opening and closing prayers.

We made several ship-wide announcements of the time and place and figured we'd get a good crowd. We even invited the captain and he said, "Sure, why not? I'll be there." But when the time came for the service only three of us were on hand, four with the captain. We shortened the service a bit, bid our goodbyes and don't believe we ever held another church service.

*   *   *

About the same time that I reported aboard the *Manatee*, another Sailor appeared—Rick Bari. For him, the *Manatee* assignment was a form of punishment. "I was ordered to the USS *Manatee* after flunking out of ET "A" school," he said. "It was early in 1962. I'll never forget ETCM Niese there on Treasure Island in San Francisco Harbor in his dismissal of me. He said, "We're sending you to sea as a deck ape and you'll regret not passing the course for becoming an ET."

101

Bari, continuing his story, said, "I still remember the nervousness that I experienced when reporting aboard and wonder how stupid I looked trying to salute the flag and quarterdeck watch officer at the same time.

"I was immediately assigned to first division under the eyes of BM3 Curtis Betts. My first work station was the forecastle and I gained great knowledge in the removal of old paint for the anchor winch. I also became somewhat of an expert in the application of various paints and protective coatings."

*   *   *

Larry McIntosh was aboard the *Manatee* at that time as well. He said he remembers making four cruises to the Far East during his tour on the ship from late 1959 through February 1963. Coming from farm life in rural Kansas where he rarely ventured far from his home, he said traveling the world was rather breathtaking.

"There were many experiences during this time," he said. "But what I remember most was a particular 1962 refueling operation while in the Western Pacific. An aircraft carrier was alongside and we had started the refueling operation when something terrible happened. Our helmsman dozed off, allowing the two ships to start coming together. When the correction was made, the sterns of the ships got very close.

"In fact, the collision alarm was sounded and the boatswain's mate announced for all hands to clear the port side and stand by for impact. Fortunately, they didn't touch. No doubt about it, however, it was very, very close. But it wasn't over just yet.

"As the ships parted, they over-corrected and the separation became too great for the winch lines and hoses to reach. They had to implement an emergency break-away and all three station rigs dropped into the water. Everything had to be reeled in. Once that was done the carrier came back alongside and we started the whole refueling procedure over again."

McIntosh said he never did find out what happened to the helmsman, who was the cause of the whole mishap, but he expected it wasn't nice.

*   *   *

Things weren't that pleasant for Leon Matiyow either. No, this BTMM had nothing to do with the refueling incident, but his troubles did start to mount when he went on ship's liberty in Sasebo, Japan. Barely 20 at the time, he was coaxed into the Enlisted Men's Club on the base, and with *Manatee* shipmates at his side, given some of that not-for-anyone-under-21 brew.

Sipping some, he smacked his lips and said, "Hey, this stuff's not half bad."

Of course, he asked for more. And more is just what he got. But with it came these two burley MPs who bodily pulled him up from his chair and asked to see his ID. Sheepishly, he complied. Then, no sooner was it determined that he was underage, that they slipped on some handcuffs and led him out the door. Of course, by this time all of Matiyow's so-called friends had scattered—some to other parts of the bar, others outside.

"We don't know this guy," one said.

"Never seen him before," another said.

"He just wandered in here on his own."

Matiyow thought the end was near. But just as soon as he was led outside it was revealed that the MPs weren't MPs at all, but *Manatee* Sailors. It was all, of course, a big joke. Regardless, for Matiyow it was the last of his brew tasting that day.

Matiyow, who served aboard ship from 1961 to 1963, said he loved his duty. "Tending the ship's boilers, particularly when the ship was getting underway, was a treat," he said. "But, after being stuck in the underbelly of the ship for long periods of time, it was also a joyous occasion to head topside for midday lunch. Just to feel the warm sun in your face before entering the mess hall was enough to make your day."

Evidently, ship duty was in Matiyow's blood. For, 18 years after he left the Navy he re-entered it, retiring E-6 with 22-and-a-half years of service.

On November 2, 1962 it was the end of another assignment for Captain Trum. He was replaced by Captain John E. Tuttle.

Now, About Those "Dear John" Letters

 It's a fact: many *Manatee* sailors, at sea for long periods of time, have both sent and received "Dear John" letters. Their contents have, of course, been long lost to the ages. Here, however, are two that may have survived:

Dear John,
I can no longer continue our relationship. The distance between us is simply too great. I must admit that I have cheated on you twice since you've been gone. Please return the picture of me that I sent you. — Love, Sue

Dear Sue,
I'm so sorry, but I can't quite remember who you are. I've enclosed some photos. Please take your picture from the pile and send the rest back to me. — Take care, John

Dear Ex-Wife Mary,
Don't try to find me. When I arrive in port next I will be asking your sister Carla to marry me. I've already arranged for a few days leave and rented a little cabin in the mountains for our honeymoon.
Have a great day! — Your ex-husband John

Dear ex-husband John,
I don't know if I ever told you this, but my sister Carla was born Carl. I hope that's not a problem.
Have a great honeymoon, — Your ex-wife Sue

CHAPTER 15

1963 THE *MANATEE'S* BIGGEST ADVENTURE

For me (Joe Kraus), the most exciting thing that happened to the *Manatee* while I was aboard was the cruise in 1963 to Australia. With our new commanding officer, Captain John E. "Jack" Tuttle, and Executive Officer Lieutenant Commander A. R. "Ken" Kenworthy aboard, the *Manatee* was one of seven ships chosen to visit the Down-Under country to help commemorate the nation's Coral Sea Celebration, April 29 through May 13. And what a trip it was.

Captain Tuttle

The entire cruise consisted of this: From Long Beach, California, the ship stopped at Pearl Harbor in the Hawaiian Islands and then went to Brisbane, Australia, then to Sydney, Australia. The next port of calls were Guam in the Mariana Islands, then Subic Bay in the Philippine Islands and Hong Kong. Later it was to the ports of Sasebo, Nagoya, Yokosuka and Hakodate in Japan. From this point there was one more stop, this one in Buckner Bay in Okinawa before once again heading home.

The worst part of the trip, however, was April 19, 1963. That was the day we crossed the equator on the way to Australia. Those of us aboard, including me, who had never crossed it before (or couldn't prove it if we had) were warned that it wouldn't be pleasant. It wasn't.

It started off with a change of names. We were the Pollywogs—those of us, officers and crew alike, who would have to go through some initiation ceremonies. On the other side were the Shellbacks—those who had previously crossed the equator and had gone through the ceremony in years past.

You knew there was trouble ahead when you took a look at the lunch menu. The Shellbacks had steak, an assortment of vegetables, soup, salad and dessert. Those of us designated Pollywogs were offered sea weed au jus (cold spaghetti with green food coloring) as the main course. Then there was blood of the red eyed sea dog (tomato juice with hot sauce), jelly fish sandwiches and last week's left over coffee, among other "delicacies."

Then there were the ceremonies themselves which consisted of so-called "operations" where they would douse you with all sorts of "medicines." This would be followed by some water hosing, and worst of all, some paddling as you ran through an endless line of Sailors on both sides of a walkway. Yikes—I hate to even think about the details. It may have lasted minutes, but at the time it seemed like hours. And, because we were in the middle of nowhere, there was no place to hide. Somehow we all survived, and for putting up with all the miseries, were presented with an official certificate, a royal dinner that evening and a top-side movie.

Our discomforts, however, were not over. Five days out of Brisbane, Australia, on April 24 the *Manatee* ran into some very bad weather. Not only was the ship battered by gale-force winds and 40-foot waves, but the waves washed away several gear lockers, life lines and deck stanchions. It even stripped away some of the ship's paint. And, if that wasn't enough to contend with, the *Manatee* had to refuel four destroyers and an aircraft carrier during the ordeal.

Once in Australian waters, the entire Australian experience was to last for a month from April 13 to May 13, 1963. The contingent of U.S. ships split off in groups of two or three, heading for various ports. Both the *Manatee* and the submarine *Blueback* were to be the official visitors to Brisbane, the first of our two stops in Australia.

Among our U.S. and Australian friendship efforts was a visit by *Manatee* crew members at two local orphanages. On tap was the offering to show the Disney movie, *101 Dalmatians* to the residents of both groups. So I, along with T. T. McCray of the supply department and Herbert V. Cunningham from the electrical division, volunteered for the assignment.

With the car and driver furnished, the three of us, along with all the equipment, left the *Manatee* about 4 p.m. First stop was the Crippled Children's Home. Before the movie we talked to a large number of the kids and their caretakers about America and the U.S. Navy, and at their request, gave out numerous autographs. At the end of the movie they all gave us very loud "Hip, Hip Hurray" cheers.

Following that visit we continued on with our driver to St. Vincent's Home, where we were met by a number of the nuns. After greeting us they escorted us to the area where the movie was to be shown and where a very large group of kids had already been waiting for us. Others came and filled the empty seats after our arrival.

We sat on a bench toward the back amongst several of them. And, once again, all three of us answered repeated questions concerning not only the ship, but about America in general. When the movie was over, the kids filed out of the room in single file, each offering their own individual "thank you" as they went by. Once the kids had returned to their rooms the nuns treated the three of us to refreshments, where we answered many more questions about us, the Navy and America.

Of course, the residents of both orphanages were invited to our open house the next day. The local media covered the open house and one of our crew—Seaman Andrew Griffiths—got his picture in the paper, in which he was shown helping one of the children. Several *Manatee* crew members donated their time giving tours. And, following this, the kids were each given presents brought from the United States.

The general public also had an opportunity to visit both the *Manatee* and the submarine *Blueback* during the three-day open house period. The residents were also treated to the music of the U.S. Pacific Fleet Band as it marched through the streets to the city hall where it gave a free hour-long concert.

From Brisbane, located in the central eastern part of the country and with about a million in population at that time, *Manatee* now was off to Sydney, nearly 500 miles further south. It was, and still is, Australia's largest city and at that time it had around four million people. Here, the ship was moored at Garden Island in the famed Sydney Harbor.

Among the first official duties, *Manatee's* Captain Tuttle presented a plaque and a key to the City of Long Beach (the *Manatee's* home port), to J. H. Luscombe, Sydney's town clerk. He had accepted the gifts of friendship on behalf of the lord mayor who was suffering from influenza at the time.

In my case, I knew there would be a limited time to see the sights. So I decided to ask for some vacation days in Sydney and got them. But I found out soon enough that there was one obstacle to that and it wasn't anything to do with the Navy. It was getting a hotel room.

To my astonishment, however, the first five hotels told me that they were full and that no rooms were available. It was only when, seeing my frustration, a patron in the last hotel lobby told me what was going on. Yes, there were hotel rooms available. But no, they wouldn't rent to me because I was a Sailor off the American ship. And, my informant said, they wouldn't rent to me because they thought I wouldn't be using the room for sleeping, but for other purposes. As a result, I ended up at the local YMCA.

I remember exploring the shops in the downtown area, experiencing the eateries and reading the local newspaper. I visited the zoo as I wanted not only to see the kangaroos, but the koala bears. And getting up close and personal to the latter was a kick. In the evening I managed to get a ticket to a live theater production of, would you believe, the American play *Showboat*. Can you picture Australian accents trying to get it right with those Southern accents? What an experience!

Earlier I had contacted the local Boy Scout office, and because I had been an assistant scoutmaster at home, I thought I might be able to visit a local troop meeting. To my astonishment not only did they say yes, but the scoutmaster involved with one of the troops invited me to have dinner with his family before the meeting.

At dinner the topic was politics and the newly elected U.S. President John F. Kennedy, whom they admired. Later, at the scout meeting, the boys insisted on a question-and-answer period. They brought out a world map and I had to point out the location of Portland, Oregon, where I lived. The questions from the scouts ranged from what we Americans liked to eat, hamburgers and fries, to what comic books I read—Tarzan and Superman. They could relate to that.

After all that, I asked if they would do me a favor. That was, to show me in the Australian night sky the famed Southern Cross. This is the southern constellation that lies in the path of the Milky Way and that can't be seen in the United States. They explained, as they showed me in the night sky, the four bright stars form a small but distinct cross. The long axis, they said, points almost exactly to the  South Pole. It's this Southern Cross that is represented on the flags of Australia, New Zealand and Western Samoa.

Four months later, as my term of enlistment was nearly over, I seriously considered re-enlisting on the condition of being stationed in the Mediterranean. After visiting places in the Western Pacific, new and exciting spots in Europe and North Africa sounded mighty interesting. But, after considering it carefully, I didn't. I left active duty and headed off to college in California. This was followed by a career in journalism, marriage, three kids and a half dozen grandkids to date.

None of this I regretted. Little did I know at the time, that should I have re-enlisted, I would have soon been right in the middle of the Vietnam War. My Mediterranean assignment, even if I had gotten that opportunity, would surly have been revoked.

*　　*　　*

The Australian visit now completed, the *Manatee* headed north to Guam in the Mariana Islands, followed by Subic Bay in the Philippines and then to Buckner Bay in Okinawa. It was in Buckner Bay that four first class midshipmen from three different NROTC units and the Naval Academy came aboard. One of these midshipmen was Richard Kalyn who said he remembers the *Manatee* well.

"The entire experience on the ship was outstanding," he said, "as the entire ship's company went out of their way to instruct and demonstrate what it took at the deck-plate level and above to execute a successful operational mission."

There was, however, an incident which he admitted he caused, that could have resulted in serious damage to the ship. It didn't. What it did result in was some serious counseling by the ship's electrical officer, Lieutenant Junior Grade Davis, the main propulsion assistant, Chief Warrant Officer Engler, and the chief engineer, Lieutenant Burkett. Midshipman Kalyn explained it this way.

"I was attempting to bring one of the ship's service turbine generators on line with the other at the main electrical switchboard. And even though I was under the supervision of the regular watch-stander, I didn't pay as close attention to his instructions as I should have. My actions resulted in a loud 'bang' and the entire ship immediately went dark. This, of course, was the entirely predictable result of trying to parallel two generators out of phase. It could have resulted in serious equipment damage or a collision if another ship had been alongside." The *Manatee* again survived one.

In September Captain Tuttle was replaced by Captain David Scott. And as for Midshipman Kalyn, he later became an engineering duty officer and in 1991 he retired from the U.S. Navy as a captain. His last duty was commanding officer, supervisor of shipbuilding, conversion and repair out of Charleston, South Carolina.

110

CHAPTER 16

1964-1966 THE HEAT IS ON ONCE AGAIN

The mid-1960s was a time when the Navy enlistments spiked. Everyone wanted to join the Navy rather than the Army, Air Force, Coast Guard or Marine Corps. But why? The Navy brass scratched their head. A study was conducted. Alas, the answer.

It was all due to a television show called *McHale's Navy*. It ran from 1962 to 1966 and then forever afterwards in TV re-runs. The show was ABCs must-see comedy series about the misadventures of a misfit PT boat crew during World War II. It actually was one of the best fighting crews in the Navy, but would break regulations when it suited them.

The conversations went something like this. Captain Binghamton: "Commander, how would you and your men like two weeks with nothing to do but play gin rummy, go surfing, have luaus with steel drum bands, dancing girls? What do you think?"

Lieutenant Commander Quinton McHale: "Two whole weeks. Wow! Oh, that'd be a wonderful change sir. Yes sir."

Captain Binghamton: "Knock it off McHale. That's what you do every week."

Ernest Borgnine, the star who played McHale, said the enlistments were real—all in the hopes, he said, enlistees would find in the Navy one of these laid-back outfits.

*   *   *

Now, what would you say if we tell you that the USS *Manatee* could have, and even would have, been the nucleus of what started our involvement in the Vietnam War? And now, to take it a step further, the reason it wasn't was due not to anything the *Manatee* did or didn't do, but to a miscalculation by the North Vietnamese. That is the assertion being made by an officer who served on the *Manatee* at that time.

Here's what happened, as reported in various news reports, on August 4, 1964: At 8 p.m. that day the US destroyers, USS *Maddox* and the USS *C. Turner Joy* (DD-951), operating in the Gulf of Tonkin, intercepted radio messages from the North Vietnamese. The impression was that an attack was imminent on the ships by several PT boats. The ships immediately called for air support from the nearby carrier, USS *Ticonderoga* (CV-14).

Within minutes eight Crusader jets appeared overhead where they were joined by ship lookouts searching for any evidence of the advancing PT boats. Mostly due to the pitch darkness, no PT boats were found and the warplanes returned to their base. The lookouts, as well, relaxed, thinking all was well. Not so. At 10 p.m., sonar operators reported torpedoes approaching. The ships, in turn, immediately maneuvered in zigzag formation to avoid disaster. And, at the same time, both ships began firing in the direction of the oncoming craft.

Two hours into the fighting, the U.S. ships reported sinking at least two, probably three of the Vietnamese boats. And, as reports of the attack reached Washington, President Lyndon B. Johnson, along with his security team, decided to retaliate with targets already in mind on North Vietnam's mainland. Known as the Gulf of Tonkin Resolution, the authorization for war was unanimously approved by Congress.

Meanwhile, back on the two destroyers, officials there now said they began to question the whole ordeal. Were there any enemy boats? Did any get sunk? Were the blips on the radar scope just "freak weather effects?" Were those torpedoes in the water just due to "overeager radar operators?" And, of course, there was another question: Just who fired first? Up to that time the rule was that the U.S. couldn't fire unless fired upon.

Once it was established that the North Vietnamese fired first, the doors opened for the U.S. to send troops into the war zone. But, was this action proof by any doubt? Was it time now for some second thoughts and a cover story to protect themselves, should a slip-up have occurred?

Observers on the *Manatee*, however, had no doubt what happened. That's because when the *Manatee* and the destroyers were docked in port, one look toward the *Maddox* and it was obvious a shooting match had occurred. The *Maddox* was riddled with bullets, some saying they were the size of grapefruits. Why then, did the destroyers hatch up this wild tale that maybe there was no enemy at all?

Now, how does all of this involve the *Manatee*? The *Manatee* officer, who said he would like to remain anonymous, said that it was years later, long after he had retired, that the PT boat incident was brought up by a retired U.S. intelligence agent. The shooting incident, he was told, was, in fact, real. But the attack on the two destroyers by the North Vietnamese was not planned. The attack, in fact, was to take on the U.S. oiler, the *Manatee* (that's us, of course), which was less inclined to shoot back with the same force as were the two destroyers. The *Manatee* was on point, refueling the two destroyers, but after refueling, turned and went in the other direction. When the PT boats arrived they faced not the *Manatee*, as planned, but the two destroyers. For the *Manatee*: great! For the North Vietnamese: a bummer.

All of this assertion of the *Manatee*'s unintended involvement is, of course, not confirmed. And there is nothing that has officially been released to the public that substantiates it. But nevertheless, it certainly makes sense. Historically it may be of no concern if it was the *Manatee* or the destroyers who were involved. The result was the same. The shooting match marked the escalation of American involvement in Southeast Asia. And after the incident, hundreds of ships were deployed to the Western Pacific, joining the *Manatee* which was already there. And the big change for the Sailors aboard ship was the fact that those normal six-month cruises turned into eight and sometimes nine months away from homeports.

During this period the *Manatee* operated mainly in the South China Sea, replenishing the ships of the 7th Fleet on patrol in that area. It was all in support of the struggle against communist aggression in Vietnam. As it turned out, however, it was a war that America and its allies, as strong as they were, never had a chance of winning.

*   *   *

Seaman Doug Bowie, who later made boatswain mate 3 and then boatswain mate 2, was on the *Manatee* in those days from 1963 to 1966. "The only good side to it was that in being in the war zone we got combat pay," Bowie said. "But the worse part by far was seeing all those body bags. They were high-lined over to us from other ships and it certainly was depressing."

Bowie was assigned to the first division, but after about 18 months he was transferred to the second division. After so many years memories tend to fade a bit, but what he said he does remember vividly was that at a stop in Pearl Harbor on the way to Japan it was announced that a new enlisted men's club was opening. To celebrate they had some special pricing—mixed drinks 10 cents, beer 5 cents.

*   *   *

As bad as things were for the *Manatee* in those years, according to some observers, it got worse when Seaman Ray Hooper reported aboard in 1964 as the ship's cook. A party animal and an always-in-trouble Sailor, Hooper was the typical central casting Sailor. But don't let me influence your thinking. Here he is with his own words.

"There was a time that Doug Bowie and I and a few other shipmates were returning to the ship and we had a confrontation with this Sailor from another ship. We all jumped on him and set about

114

showing him that you just don't mess with the *Manatee* boys.

"Let's see. There were six of us and only one of him. So if you think you know who was winning that disagreement, think again. It wasn't us. But about that time Lieutenant L. O. Chase came upon us, and after observing what was going on, he said to us, 'Way to go, heroes! Do you think that I need to send a working party out here to help you boys? Now, get your (expletive deleted) back to the ship.'

"I don't know who was happier, the guy by himself who was fighting us, or the five or six of us who were making fools of ourselves. At any rate, we went back to the ship and nothing was ever said about the matter."

Of course, there was the time after a night on the town that Hooper was being carried back to the ship on the shoulders of Boatswain Mate Third Class Ray Settle. Settle didn't quite get Hooper aboard, dumping him instead off the gangway. We're not sure if it was his first or second baptism.

And then there was the time Hooper took from the ship's kitchen this 10 pound turkey, hiding it under his clothes as he passed by the quarterdeck watch. It seems that 10 or 15 shipmates and Hooper had rented this house down around the Pike area in Long Beach. They, of course, didn't have much to eat. They had spent all their money on beer, wine, whiskey and other such necessities. Was he a Good Samaritan or thief? *Manatee* historians may be pondering this question for some time.

Hooper's big caper, however, has been a secret all these years—until now. So, should you have connections to the Naval Investigation Service, CIA or any other such organization, Hooper says, with a smile, that this is nothing but a sea story, told by a lying old Sailor. Believe that, and like the old saying, we'll sell you some oceanfront property in Arizona.

So, here's Hooper: "The *Manatee* was sailing somewhere in and around the South China Sea when I and another stew burner (ship's cooks) decided to do away with the ships bell. It was an old Navy tradition that the ships cooks were responsible for shining the ships bell. How the deck apes ever thought that up is beyond me. But anyway to be quite frank with you, that old bell could really turn green from the salt spray and all.

"But, anyway, my buddy and I decided that if we threw the bell over the side that would be the end of that tradition and a lot of hard work. Well, we carried out our mission and after a week or so someone noticed that the bell was missing. The captain was told, and needless to say, all hell broke out about that bell. The old man got on the PA system and told the crew that if the ship's bell didn't show up that all the crew's liberty would be secured until it did show up.

"Well, we were at sea and would be for quite a while, so that threat was not a big thing. But, as we got closer to getting back into port, my cohort in this little incident started to get scared and worried. He thought that since the crew's liberty would be secured that maybe we should fess up to our doings. He said he knew in the end we would be caught anyway.

"I was not very smart back in those days, but I wasn't completely dumb. By admitting guilt, the crew would go on liberty and guess where we would go? I had no choice. I threatened great bodily harm if he talked. Of course, I was kidding, but he didn't know that.

"To my dismay, my buddy kept his mouth shut and the whole deal blew over. And somewhere during this tour of duty the ship got another bell and the old tradition of the ships cook having the duty of shining the bell remained. So much for fighting the good fight."

Hooper admitted that he got into a scrape or two during his two years aboard the *Manatee*. It included several captain's masts and one court-marshal, but it all worked out in the end. That was due, he said, to some intervention by CS-2 Cleophis Jackson who tried to turn his life around.

"Old Jack would tell me a line that went like this, 'When a man is a fool and he knows he's a fool, he has a chance to change things. But when a man is a fool and he thinks that everyone around him is a fool, then he is screwed for good as long as he thinks like that."

116

Hooper said this was poetry to his ears. "Here I was 21 or 22 years old, five years in the Navy and a seaman, a rate grabber for sure. I was doing all the wrong things and couldn't figure out why the Navy and all those petty officers were always picking on me.

"But, finally, the light that Jackson was trying to show me clicked on and I started to do the things I was supposed to do. And, all at once, no one was picking on me anymore. I kept trying to look good in Jackson's eyes and at the same time everything started to improve for me in the Navy."

Hooper said that after Jackson's intervention, he kept himself squared away. Then, after many duty stations, he was promoted to master chief petty officer, retiring after 30 years total service time. "God bless you Jack, and again, thank you for helping change my life."

*　　*　　*

It should be noted here that Sailors throughout history got into minor trouble from time to time and situations had to be dealt with right away aboard ship. There were no lawyers and no one had six months to a year to prepare a case. A day or two was pushing it. Otherwise things could get out of hand rather quickly. Fear of the consequences of their actions may have been the norm. But in reality punishments weren't all that severe. That may be because the ship's executive officers and captains may remember, in the back of their mind, their own transgressions.

That fact, however, wasn't general knowledge among the crew. Just ask Dan McCarville. He was a third class shipfitter and served aboard the *Manatee* from 1965 to 1967. One of his best friends at the time was Edward Clinton Caldwell, a seaman assigned to the same engineering department.

"At the time we were both working on correspondence courses," McCarville said. "Because of that we needed to concentrate and shut out all the noise which seemed to surround us at all times. So, we thought, what better place to study than to go to the carpentry shop, located near the front of the ship.

"We waited until late at night and it was pitch dark.  Not thinking, we both took out a cigarette lighter and lit cigarettes as we walked forward, the lighters plainly seen by the lookouts and the captain, which at that time was on the bridge. In several areas of the ship it was absolutely forbidden to smoke due to the dangerous conditions, particularly within range of the highly flammable aviation gas stored in our tanks. We knew the rules well, but we just weren't thinking.

"Well, it turns out we found ourselves facing severe penalties, even court-martials for an offense the regulations state as 'Hazardous Actions toward a Naval Vessel.' At the appointed time I was standing outside the captain's cabin, Caldwell right behind me. The captain called me in first. I stood as he reviewed my service record. Nothing was said for some time. Then the captain said, 'I see here that you hail from Fort Dodge, Iowa. That's my hometown as well. Tell you what, this case is dismissed. But don't let me hear from you anymore. And oh, by the way, tell your partner he is dismissed as well.'

"I, of course, couldn't believe what I just heard. Both Caldwell and I could have been stripped of our ranks, even booted out of the Navy. Needless to say our smoking days were over."

McCarville went on to make a career in the Navy, retiring 27 years later as a damage control chief. He has since, however, lost track of his best friend Caldwell. And, after searching for him for more than 20 years, he has no idea what happened to him.

*   *   *

If you want to be reassured that captains were far from perfect just ask Larry Milburn who served aboard the *Manatee* for about four years in the early 1960s, and during that time, received many commendations on the way he handled his duties.

One of those duties was serving as a gig coxswain. His responsibilities were in full swing when the ship was anchored and the ship's motorboats were in use to ferry crewmembers to and from the shore. The captain, of course, had his own special boat for such occasions, the captain's gig, and the gig coxswain was the one in charge of running it.

"On one of our trips overseas we were anchored out in the harbor of Hong Kong," Milburn said. "I took the captain ashore. He told me to pick him up around midnight. When he boarded the boat I noticed he was a little tipsy and had a woman with him. Women at that time were not authorized aboard U.S. Navy ships unless, of course, the occasion was an open house. This was no open house.

"When we got close to the ship, he came out of his cabin and she followed him. He then told me that he would take over control of the craft. I told him that the waters were rough and the craft was difficult to handle. But he informed me that he was the captain. Then, with him in control, we soon were approaching the ship, but much faster than we should have. The result was the small boat smashed into the gangway.

"At this time, the captain turned to me and said, 'Larry, why don't you take it from here.' I did, and as the captain and his friend were leaving the boat, he told me to put an early call in. He wanted her off the ship before the crew got up."

Milburn said he served under several *Manatee* captains and he wasn't about to reveal which of these captains was the subject of this story. None were like the Captain Bligh, depicted in the book and movie, *Mutiny on the Bounty*. But nether were any perfect.

*   *   *

In charge of the *Manatee* from September 28, 1964, to September 1, 1965, was Captain Benjamin Hill Stough Jr. He in turn would be relieved by Captain S. W. Gaiennie on September 1, 1965, and serve until September 1967, when Captain Evans King would officially take the reins.

119

Meeting
And
Greeting
The Locals

ABOVE: Unless you know the language, signs identifying the stores don't help much. But it doesn't take long to find the most interesting ones to visit. LEFT: Adults in foreign lands often shy away from U.S Sailors with a camera. Those who didn't get the word are these kids in the streets of Hong Kong. TOP LEFT: The most popular game with kids in Japan-backyard baseball.

CHAPTER 17

1967 ATTENTION SICK BAY:
READY OR NOT—HERE WE COME!

Manatee Sailors, away from their families for months at a time, often were more than a little lax in writing home. And, as might be expected, family members back home were more than a little worried at times concerning those family members serving sea duty in the military. So, when those stateside letters weren't answered, they wrote the ship's commanding officer. All had the same questions, Where are you? What is the ship doing? Is my son, brother or husband OK?

With more things to do than answer letters, over the years the captains decided enough was enough. So, about four times a year they wrote one letter that was duplicated and sent to all the families back home, regardless if their son, brother or husband was writing home on a regular basis or not.

The letters were mostly upbeat, fun things like saying the ship went here and visited there and work things like rendezvous with X number of other ships at sea. The letters covered the basics, but with little detail. But, occasionally there was mention about things that were a little more worrisome. As an example, here are some of those letters sent out in 1967 by the *Manatee's* commanding officer at that time, Captain Evans King.

"… *Manatee* expects to be in port in Long Beach from the 24th of March until deployment on the 12th of April. During this period the ship will be preparing for overseas deployment. I have urged the men of *Manatee* to ensure that their various legal and personal business has been taken care of before departure…"

Of course, these families had only to pick up any newspaper or turn on their TV at home to find out that there was a war going on in the area the ship was heading. It wasn't mentioned in the letter to have a will made out or life insurance. Some families, however, just might have had that in mind. To make matters worse, there was this:

"... If an emergency situation should arise while *Manatee* is deployed, you should contact the Navy Relief. This organization exists to render assistance to Navy families in times of crisis..."

But, if that wasn't enough, there was this: "On our way to Hong Kong, Typhoon Carla decided to come over northern Luzon and head right across our course. Even after Carla had passed us the seas were quite rough and we took occasional rolls of 20 degrees..."

After leaving Hong Kong, the captain wrote more bad news. "... Typhoon Diane threatened to disrupt operations in the Tonkin Gulf. All ships took evasive action. However, since fuel becomes a particularly critical asset in bad weather, the *Manatee* continued to ply its trade. We had one very rough day but worked around the clock to fuel our customers..."

If that wasn't enough there was this: "... After two days in Subic (The Philippines) loading for our return trip, we departed for Yokosuka (Japan) and had a typhoon to contend with. Gilda was east of the Philippines and headed directly across our path..."

Then, once again: "... In order to make up for the days we lost (dealing with the aforementioned typhoons) we took the direct route from Yokosuka (Japan) to Long Beach. This northern route is not noted for good weather at this time of year and we soon found ourselves on a rock and roll ocean.

"... We diverted course to assist with refueling operations with the aircraft carrier *Kitty Hawk* and two destroyers. We decided to send our mail with them, which would ensure its delivery a week before we reached Long Beach.

"The sea was still pretty rough with a cross swell that made us all roll. Then, in the process of transferring our mail to a destroyer we had one of the few mishaps of the cruise. A large swell caused the *Manatee* and the destroyer to roll towards each other. The highline suddenly slacked by this roll, dipping the transfer bag into the water.

"The force of the sea tore a hole in the transfer bag and our mail, neatly packaged in an orange mail bag, went floating off astern. With a carrier and destroyer hooked up fueling, we could not stop to attempt recovery. In fact we were steaming away at 12 knots. It was still black as pitch with an hour to go before sunrise. We feared that our mail would be delivered directly to Davy Jones' Locker.

"Although the prospects of recovery were slim we were determined to try. We told *Kitty Hawk* of our problem and as soon as it was light a helicopter and a destroyer were sent back along our track. With luck and the superior search capability of the helicopter our mail bag was recovered and returned to us. Everything was wet but most of the mail was salvageable."

The captain wrote that, despite the safe return of the mail bag, the challenges with the weather still remained. He continued: "... The weather by now had shifted around to our bow and the winds were up to gale force. We had to slow down considerably to prevent damage to the ship from pounding seas. For three days we had to poke along with a weather front moving along just ahead of us, messing up the ocean in our path. ...It was a very rough trip by any standard."

What the captain didn't mention was just how many shipmates suffered from the effects of seasickness and the long lines seeking help from the ship's medical team. It was the last *Manatee* letter he had to write as he was replaced in September 1967 by Captain Evans King.

*   *   *

CHAPTER 18

1968 *MANATEE* "DRAFTED"
FOR NEW VIETNAM WAR MISSION

In times of both peace and war the *Manatee* had carted oil to the ships at sea. But with the conflict warming up more than just a notch in Vietnam, the ship was virtually drafted for an added mission—to carry ammunition to the war zone. This, of course, was in addition to its regular mission of delivering fuel. Somewhere along the way, however, groceries were added to the shopping list. The *Manatee* was beginning to look like, not just a gas station, a gun and ammunition shop and a supermarket, but an entire shopping center.

The 1968 tour began on May 14, just two weeks after *Manatee's* new commanding officer, Captain John F. Gillooly, reported aboard. Then the *Manatee* traded Long Beach for Subic Bay in the Philippines as a homeport. This trip away from the states would last seven months. The ship made all of the 315 replenishment commitments it was scheduled for during this time.

Just what happens in a typical replenishment detail at sea is best described by the editors of the *Manatee's* 1968 cruise book. Here, in an abbreviated form, is how the editors described the process.

"First the *Manatee's* radio room receives a message that a ship or ships need replenishment. Then the message is quickly routed to each department for preparation work. The deck force checks the fueling rigs and cargo transfer rig required by the receiving ship. Winches are tested and dozens of lines required for the evolution are laid out on deck.

"On the tank deck, the ship fitters and damage control men set up the proper alignment to transfer fuel in the jungle of pipes, tanks and valves. Valves are tested, hose fittings are secured and cargo pumps warmed with steam.

"In the main engine control room and the fire room extra men are brought on duty to keep close watch on the steam pressures and temperatures crucial to running the ship at cruising speed while employing numerous steam winches and steam pumps.

"Supply department store keepers break out groceries and spare parts ordered by the receiving ship and ready them on the cargo deck for highline transfer. On the bridge, a quartermaster takes the helm and phone talkers link the bridge with every part of the ship.

"When the captain is satisfied that all stations are properly manned and ready he orders the signal bridge to hoist the Romeo flag close up, which signals the receiving ship that she is now authorized to come alongside.

"The approach is closely watched as the 100 feet separating the ships allows little margin for error. Once the customer ship is in position shot lines or bolos are passed by *Manatee's* gunners mates and from the attached messenger lines, the rigs are drawn over.

"When the rigging is completed on the other ship a signal is given, and valves are opened on *Manatee*, and the three cargo pumps begin to deliver fuel at a rate of 1,000 gallons per minute.

"Meanwhile, the cargo rig has been passed to the other ship. Cargo and ammunition are delivered by Burton rig, where winches on both ships provide the power. For safety, personnel must be transferred by a manila highline manned entirely by the crews of the ships. On the smaller ships, even groceries and mail are transferred by this latter method.

"Mail is the most eagerly anticipated commodity, since for many ships oilers are the only postmen during an arduous 20-30 day period at sea.

"Ammunition is transferred to the gunfire support ships and retrograde, expended ammunition casings and carrying pallets, is passed to *Manatee* for transit back to port and reuse.

"When all fuel and supplies have been transferred, the hoses, wires and lines are recovered aboard *Manatee* and another cus-

126

tomer steams from alongside. Before the crew can rest though, the rigs must be readied for the next replenishment."

*   *   *

All of this, of course, is if everything goes off without a hitch. But that wasn't the case on August 9, 1968, when the *Manatee* was refueling the USS *Tripoli* (LPH-10) on one side and the USS *Thomaston* (LSD-28) on the other. All was going well when alarms went off on the *Tripoli* as one of its men engaged in the refueling operations fell overboard. At that point everything came to a halt as phone talkers on all ships spread the news.

There were major concerns, particularly with the man in the drink who helplessly watched as all three ships, including his own, continued for parts unknown. As everyone knows, you can't stop multi-ton ships on a dime. So, when things did come to a halt a small boat was launched from the *Tripoli* and the fallen seaman (who was wearing a life jacket) was recovered.

*   *   *

If all of this refueling business and correcting some missteps sounds like a lot of work, it was. But there was a little bit of fun as well. On Sundays in 1968, for instance, the ship held skeet shoots on the fantail and boxing matches on the main deck. All of this was followed by a barbecue on the fantail.

During the noon hour some members of the crew built up their tans stretching out on the forecastle or fantail. In the evenings some participated in table games and playing musical instruments such as guitars and harmonicas. And there was usually a movie, most often held outside on the top deck—a walk-in drive-in, of sorts. But bad weather didn't stop a movie. The projectionist just moved his operations inside to the enlisted mess.

There were good deeds. Like when V. A. Cortez Jr., the *Manatee's* cook, learned that the destroyer USS *Camp* (DE-251) was about to celebrate its 25th birthday. So, when the ship pulled alongside for refueling, Cortez sent over a freshly baked cake. It had to be high-lined over and was nearly engulfed in the waves midway in transit. But it made it safely without getting wet.

And there was the time that year that the *Manatee* crew learned that a children's hospital in Kaohsiung, Taiwan, was in need of help. So, working under the direction of *Manatee's* Lieutenant Junior Grade Jim Milton, eleven *Manatee* Sailors that included Seamen L. A. Krogen, L. P. Seilinski, John A. Haschke, Clements, and Kuebel spent their liberty painting several rooms at the hospital. Surplus items on board the *Manatee* were given to the hospital, as well. This included a medical instrument sterilizer, a water heater and a refrigerator. To top it off, the entire crew of the *Manatee* donated several hundred dollars to help in the hospital's work. Most of the youngsters in the hospital were suffering from the crippling effects of polio and were in the facility for therapy and corrective surgery.

*   *   *

Charles "Mike" Tunstall, who was aboard the *Manatee* 1968-1969, said he remembers Kaohsiung as well, but it was for more than those good deeds at the hospital. "We did visit a few bars there and what I remember most about these visits was how beautiful the women were," he said. "But," he admitted, "these memories might have been shaped a little due to the number of brewski's we had." Tunstall didn't define what a brewski was, but it may have to do with something a little bit stronger than the Kaohsiung tap water.

Tunstall said, however, that those good memories weren't to last. This was because there was much more to be concerned about, particularly when the ship was docked in Da Nang Harbor. "We were delivering some items on short notice that were needed in Vietnam," Tunstall said. "And although we weren't directly involved in the fighting, we knew the war was still raging when we saw Agent Orange floated over the ship and the crew."

Agent Orange, of course, was used by the military to cut down dense jungle vegetation to make it safer to patrol and to root out the enemy. The effects of this chemical on humans, however, wasn't generally known at that time. And, despite a great deal of evidence, it is still debated in some circles just how much exposure to this chemical is necessary to trigger later-in-life medical issues.

*   *   *

If Agent Orange didn't get you those typhoons certainty did. "My first experience with one of these," Tunstall said, "was when we were docked in Sasebo, Japan, and the word came out that we were to head out to sea.

"The largest tanker in the world at that time was docked there and we were told that should that ship ever get loose in the typhoon, our ship would be crushed. We didn't question these orders. We left.

"I've never been seasick before, but I have been sea scared. And not only did I put on foul weather gear and a life jacket, as we were told, but on my own I added a second life jacket."

Tunstall said that during one of those typhoons he was in one end of the ship and the mess hall was on the other. "It was too dangerous for us to go anywhere, let alone the mess hall. It must have been two days before we got anything to eat".

*   *   *

Finally, Time For A Party After Many Weeks At Sea

RIGHT: Here is the Manatee crew at a ship's party held at the Wilton Hotel in Long Beach. From left are Walt "Hoot" Terrel, George Wallish, Mrs. Todd, Todd, Mrs. Lamb, Al Lamb, Earl Penno, Dan Mehner and William Bergmeister in the early 1950s. CENTER RIGHT: Belling up the bar in the mid 1960s are four Manatee sailors. The two in the center are Don Welk (left) and Ray Hooper. BOTTOM RIGHT: Having a good time here are from left: Ray Hooper and Dave Perrigoue and shipmates Ordua, Boys, Moore and Arkie in the early 1960s. TOP LEFT: Brian M. Vesper and two shipmates found someone to join the party. CENTER LEFT: A stay at Suma Beach, south of Kobe, Japan in July of 1953. From left: Douglas Hurn and Paul Jack Sturgill. BOTOM LEFT: According to shipmate Paul Clark, a popular hangout in Subic Bay, Philippines was the White Hat Club.

131

CHAPTER 19

1969 *MANATEE'S* BRUSH
WITH "THE KING"

What happens when you join the Navy, expecting a new adventure, but find out things just don't go quite as expected? Meet Dalton "Bill" Lunsford, a machinist mate. It was in 1969 and he had no more than reported aboard the ship when he was escorted into the interior of the ship.

"Then," as he tells it, "I saw before me a complete mess of nuts and bolts, little pieces and big pieces of something. I didn't know what it was, but before I could ask, I was told that all these pieces was once an air compressor and the guy who took it apart just got out of the Navy and had left the ship moments before. Now, I was told, it was my job to put it all back together.

"Mind you," Lunsford said, "they were very helpful. They shoved a photo of the gadget in front of me and said this is what it was supposed to look like. That was my introduction to the *Manatee*."

*   *   *

Lunsford said it was months later, while on liberty, when he discovered he was going to be late—like very late—reporting back to the ship. Knowing he was already in big trouble, he decided why not stay away longer and enjoy the extra freedom while he could. So he took up residence in one of the homes rented by a Sailor friend, assigned at the time on shore duty to serve as a military policeman.

"Ironic as it was," he said, "here I was AWOL, a wanted man, and staying in the home of a person with the responsibility of arresting me." Lunsford said the penalty he had to endure for his caper was a $100 fine and the demotion of one rank from first to second class petty officer.

*   *   *

In the 1960s, one of the biggest names in show business was one Elvis Presley. And, despite the fact that both of his parents were unemployed welfare recipients, he ended up earning $4.5 billion in his lifetime. In those early years, however, concentrating on his many recordings and movie making, 33 in all, he didn't give many concerts. But one Elvis did give was in 1961, in Hawaii, where he donated the entire proceeds to help build the USS *Arizona* (BB-39) Memorial in Pearl Harbor.

The memorial, approved by President Eisenhower in 1958, was completed with both public funds and private donations and was dedicated in 1962. Now, skipping to the summer of 1969, Presley was visiting Hawaii and wanted to see the completed memorial that he helped finance.

The *Manatee* was in port at the time for repairs and had on board an admiral's barge. Much fancier than a captain's barge, this replaced the usual boat and was temporarily being used by the *Manatee* captain, at that time Captain Charles E. (Ted) Faas. So, when it was learned Presley wanted to visit the memorial, the *Manatee* obliged and offered the barge.

Now, enter one Barry Dodd, who served on the *Manatee* in 1968 -1969. "I remember the Elvis incident well," he said. "I was fortunate enough to be the engineman on the barge. And it wasn't just Presley that we picked up that day, but his wife Priscilla and Elvis's entire entourage."

This personal entourage (bodyguards) was known as the "Memphis Mafia," and was given matching rings by Elvis. The diamond and gold rings sported a thunderbolt and the letters "TCB," reportedly standing for "Take Care of Business." Elvis was buried wearing one of the rings. Dodd explained that there were five or six people in all on that round trip to the memorial that day, a trip courtesy of the *Manatee* crew.

The next day Dodd would rejoin the rest of the crew, completing repairs to the ship's whistle, testing and adjusting the cables before the *Manatee* departed for its homeport in Long Beach. For Dodd, it also meant the end of another life's journey, a much-anticipated discharge, having served his four-year enlistment.

For Elvis, he was then off to Las Vegas to begin a new leg in his life's journey—giving concerts. After Las Vegas he traveled all across the United States. There were 1,145 concerts, in fact, from 1969 to 1977. But it all came with a price. He became addicted to prescription drugs. He became overweight. Many worried about his health. Priscilla divorced him in 1973. And, just four years later, Elvis Presley would be found dead at his home in Memphis, Tennessee. He was just 42 years old.

*   *   *

Whale Boats Prove Their Worth
In Ship To Shore Transportation

BMSN Robert Walton remembers all those whale boats and motor launches in which he helped man in the early 1950s. Above, some of the Manatee crew are shown heading for liberty at Tsingtao, China. In good weather it was nice. In bad weather... well, that was another matter.

CHAPTER 20

1970-1972 FROM A FIRE TO AN OIL SPILL TO THE *MANATEE'S* RUN-IN WITH A SITTING PRESIDENT

Everyone has their bad days. For the *Manatee* crew one of those days was February 13, 1970. It all started when Electrician Mate Third Class Craig Ferguson, on watch at the time and in the ship's engine room, noted an oil leak in the number two ship's service generator.

"I immediately attempted to stop the flow of oil with my hands," he said. "But oil dripping from the ruptured gauge entered the turbine casing and ignited, causing second degree burns on my hand.

"After calling for assistance, I started spraying the area with a CO_2 extinguisher. This didn't seem to help, so I ran to get the 50-pound system. Upon my return the smoke was so intense I couldn't get near it."

In the meantime, Third Class Machinist Mate Harold Masdow reported the fire to the bridge, saying it was out of control. General quarters was sounded; a repair group sent to the scene made the decision to stop the flames with water fog and protein foam. With this and other means the fire was brought under control and moments later the fire was reported to be completely out.

Hospitalman Chief Robert F. Bice remembered the fire as well. He was serving as the ship's senior medical department representative at the time. He said that while no one was seriously hurt, the fire, among other things, knocked out power to radio central. "Earlier I had been authorized to operate a ham radio station on the ship," he said. "I ran numerous phone patches for the crew to talk to their families via amateur radio. It's a good thing, because when the ship lost communications, the amateur radio station had electrical power and established communications with 11th Naval Headquarters, alerting them of the problem."

After an official investigation it was determined that no personal error caused the fire and because of quick action by the crew and because other systems were operating properly, there was no loss of life or serious injuries. The quick action averted a major catastrophe—fire being one of the main concerns aboard ship.

*　　*　　*

Richard Nixon took the oath of office of President of the United States on January 20, 1969, and resigned from office on August 9, 1974. The general public would remember this president mostly for Watergate and all its investigations. For the *Manatee* crew, however, it would be for something entirely different.

First, let's introduce Casa Pacifica. Located halfway between San Diego and Los Angeles on the Pacific Ocean, it served as Nixon's Western White House. This "country home," a large, Spanish-style mansion, had 14 rooms and was located on 110 acres at the southernmost point of San Clemente. Sitting above one of the West Coast's major surfing spots, it had stunning views of the Pacific Ocean.

It was here that President Nixon visited with Soviet Premier Leonid Brezhnev, Mexican President Gustavo Diaz Ordaz, Japanese Prime Minister Eisaku Sato and many others, deciding most important matters of state. Then, following the President's resignation, it was here that he retired to write his memoirs. Here, also, Nixon spent many hours hiking along his favorite beach.

Now, enter the USS *Manatee*, skippered at the time by Captain Jack L. Snyder. The *Manatee*, of course, was a proud battle-tested vessel, a veteran of World War II, Korea and Vietnam, who just happened by on this nice day, August 20, 1971. The story of what happened that day is a story that Joe (he never gave his last name), the ship's boatswain of the aircraft carrier USS *Ticondero-ga*, likes to tell.

"The *Manatee* was discharging sludge from her empty tanks at the same time she was pumping fuel to us," he said. "This is called butterworthing and accomplished by running steam-jets in the tanks to clean them. At the time we were steaming along in the southern California operating area, not too far from President Nixon's Western White House in San Clemente, California.

"When the *Manatee* started discharging all of this sludge into the ocean, as you might have guessed, all of this gooey stuff washed up onto Nixon's pristine and prized beachfront."

According to news reports, the story going national, the incident was much more serious than first thought. For not only did the sludge go into the ocean, but along with it, went some 230,000 gallons of black oil. News reports said this was all happening during a refueling mission with an aircraft carrier. Then, explaining how this could take place, officials said the tank cleaning residue was fed into the refueling operations, causing a large discharge of oil under extremely high pressure.

"After an investigation, heads rolled," the report continued. "It included the *Manatee's* captain, chief engineers, the main propulsion officer, the officer of the deck and the conning officer. All were relieved from duty, or in just one word—fired."

The *Manatee* crew as well had its share of discomfort—its Sailors got some unwanted shore duty cleaning up Nixon's beach. Other volunteers also helped, the oil was not just on Nixon's beach, but had also spread on beaches leading toward San Diego.

This story was confirmed by *Manatee* Sailor Charles Lewis. "I had just been transferred to Navy Recruiting Duty in Raleigh, North Carolina, when this incident hit the news," he said. "In fact, it made headlines all over the United States. I remember at the time that I illegally used the government's telephone line and called the ship's office and talked to some of my old shipmates about it. The story then was that it was an accident."

It was determined, as part of the investigation that the accident was made worse when the ship tried to cover-up the incident. It found that although the spill was reported to the bridge of the *Manatee* by Sailors on watch, no action was taken. The *Manatee*'s captain didn't even report it to higher authorities. The spill, in fact, was first reported by a civilian vessel which spotted oil in the water off the coast. This was then traced to the *Manatee* by a destroyer crew which reported seeing oil in the *Manatee*'s wake.

Lewis said that for many years it was common practice that, after a cruise, all hands E-5 and below had to go down in the tanks and scrape the oil sludge off the bulkheads. "The sludge was thrown overboard, but we were supposed to be at least 100 miles out to sea when we did this," he said.

*   *   *

Lewis was a Yeoman 3rd Class on the *Manatee* in the early 1970s. And during that time he said he remembered a bachelor Captain C. E. Faas, who just couldn't wait to get off the ship and go on liberty. So, he said, it was this captain's custom to be the first off the ship when the *Manatee* hit a port—any port.

"One particular time I remember," Lewis said, "was when the ship had entered Subic Bay in the Philippines. I was a telephone talker on the bridge and happened to be listening when the captain called for a tug and a pilot to bring us in. He was told to hang on—like really hang on—for it would be at least three hours before they could get around to helping.

"Well, this liberty-hound captain was to have none of that. He immediately said to heck with that noise and brought the ship in himself. He did this within 50 feet or less and parallel to the pier. Then, just like in the latest John Wayne western movie, the boatswains lassoed the pier. The ropes were then hooked to the winches. This brought us up to the dock.

"Needless to say, the captain scored points that day. But as the first off the ship he didn't wait around long enough for any praise from his crew."

*   *   *

On July 1, 1970 Admiral Elmo R. Zumwalt, Jr. became the chief of naval operations. He was the youngest man to hold the post and the youngest to achieve four-star rank. His espousing of liberal policies regarding the discipline and dress of Sailors aided him in becoming one of the most controversial Chiefs of Naval Operations in history.

Admiral Zumwalt

Lewis said he remembered when this happened, and that due to Zumwalt's policies it made life on the *Manatee* and the Navy, in general, a lot friendlier as it concerned the rank and file Sailor.

"Zumwalt allowed sideburns and/or full beards within reason and immediately many Sailors on board the *Manatee* started growing sideburns or beards," Lewis said. "But our captain at the time was beside himself. He told the crew that it was restriction for them 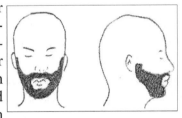 until they shaved off the offending hair. Because the captain refused to embrace any of Admiral Zumwalt's relaxed rules, he remained very unpopular with the crew."

Throughout the Navy, however, Zumwalt's unprecedented changes and his determination to bring the Navy into the modern age proved their worth when in his first year in office, first-term reenlistments rose from 10 to 17 percent. But, knowing well that his policies weren't welcome in all circles, he wasn't amiss at acknowledging it. When his tenure as chief of naval operations was over four years later, he summed up his service to an audience by saying, "I have a wonderful list of friends and a wonderful list of enemies, and am very proud of both lists."

*   *   *

Ship's Boatswain's mate, as I remember them, were hard-driving as a whole. And despite the fact they usually had a coffee cup in one hand and stood around a lot, they were pretty rough characters. For some reason, probably because they seemed to know a lot about everything and could do just about anything, they seemed to be favored by captains.

Don't just take my word for it. Take Boatswain's Mate Third Class Kenneth Ferrier as an example. He was stationed aboard the *Manatee* from 1969 through 1971. And all during this time he was a walking 'Monopoly Get-Out-Of-Jail-Free' card who could do no wrong. Here's a case in point.

"I can recall when several of my friends and me were having a really good time in this bar in Hawaii," Ferrier said. "Well, I guess I got more than a little drunk and as a result got into more than just a little trouble.

"Hearing about the big ruckus, the MPs came by and were ready to haul me away to the brig. Then I had a stroke of good luck. It was someone who came to rescue me—the captain. He talked to the MPs and convinced them that he would take care of things. And he did just that. He let me go back to the ship and sober up."

I hear tell such incidents between captains and boatswain's mate aren't uncommon. So, the question is: Do captains like boatswain's mate better? Answer: You bet!

*   *   *

A Navy tradition, started between World War I and World War II, was that whoever held the midnight to 4 a.m. watch each New Year's Day would write their ship's log report in the form of a poem. But even though it was set in rhyme, it had to include all the pertinent information of a regular log report.

Often these logs were filed away, never to be seen again. An organization called The Deck Log Project was able to save, for posterity, several of these special log reports. Among them was this one written by Ensign R. A. Dyer who served aboard the *Manatee* and held the watch on Friday, January 1, 1971. The *Manatee*, at that time, was heading to Subic Bay from Yankee Station.

Aboard the USS *Manatee*, Friday, January 1, 1971 Deck Log - Remarks sheet by Officer of the Watch Ensign R. A. Dyer

Headed for Subic after a short Tonkin swing
I absently twirl my wedding ring
And think about home and my lovely bride
Suddenly I feel cold inside.
It's New Year's Eve and I've got the deck
Binocular strap not arms around my neck
I stare at the repeater that reads One Zero Four
But not the face of the wife I adore
Boilers one, two and four are steaming tonight
And both generators spin to give power and light
The skipper is SOPA and OTC
He's Captain Jack Snyder of the *Manatee*
All ahead full with eighty four turns
Gives us sixteen even as the black oil burns
The starboard steering unit is on the line
And except for rocking we're doing just fine.
But I wonder if folks back home know we're here
As they celebrate the birth of another year
Do they even care that we're alone again?
Are they concerned only with music and gin?
Julie sits home on this New Year's Eve
But I think she knows, yes she must believe
The loneliness we feel is a small price to pay
For the honor of serving my country each day.
I'm sure tonight that all over the world
Each Sailor wants to be with his wife or girl
And I wish Julie's arms were around my neck
But it's New Year's Eve and I've got the deck.

On November 8, 1971 a new *Manatee* captain reported on board, Commander Richard H. Engelbrecht. He would serve until July 31, 1973. At that point Lieutenant Commander Robert Steven Black took over for just two weeks until August 14, 1973.

Once in port after a long period at sea, Manatee crewmen can man small boats and inspect the exterior of the ship.

CHAPTER 21

1973 THEY SAID IT WOULDN'T BE
OVER UNTIL THE FAT LADY SINGS

In show business and on opera stages around the world the saying is "It's not over until the fat lady sings." As far as we know, there were no ladies stationed aboard the *Manatee* except for that stow-a-way chicken in 1962. But, for the *Manatee* there was definitely an ending just the same.

It came on August 14, 1973, at least officially. That's the day the Navy set aside as the ship's official decommissioning ceremony. It was held at the Pier E Naval Shipyard in Long Beach, California. As was explained in the printed program of the day, "The decommissioning ceremony marks the retirement of a ship as a unit of the operating forces of the United States Navy. At the moment of covering the commission pennant, USS *Manatee* will no longer be the responsibility of the Commanding Officer who has been charged with the task of making and keeping her ready for any mission required by our nation."

The Commanding Officer, Lieutenant Commander Robert S. Black, was only a month before, assigned as the ship's skipper. He had been for two years the ship's executive officer.

This day, however, with the ship's crew in attendance, Lieutenant Commander Black gave some closing words followed by remarks by Captain Roland A. Bowlin, Commander Service Group One. The colors were then lowered, the benediction said, and then for a final good-bye, there was a lone trumpet, slowly playing a last and final taps. The USS *Manatee* at that moment and as far as the Navy was concerned, was no more.

*   *   *

The *Manatee*, however, didn't die easily. It sat at the Long Beach shipyards for a period of four months. Empty and abandoned and totally unguarded, one *Manatee* former shipmate happened upon it by accident, saying to himself the ship before him looked remarkably like the one he was on in his Navy days. On further examination he saw the familiar markings—AO-58 on the bow.

"What a kick," he said to himself. So he dropped everything and walked on to the pier. Then, seeing the gangplank, he climbed it and walked aboard, fully expecting a guard. But not one was on hand. So he started walking—all through the ship, each passageway, each compartment bringing back memories.

Bill Lunsford, on the ship from 1969 to 1970, said he found out later that the ship was used during those four months as a location for several films and TV shows. He said on one occasion he spotted the ship on TV. "I saw action scenes in the ship's engine room, shots fired, chase scenes—all on our old ship."

＊　　　＊　　　＊

According to Jim Osenton, who was aboard the ship for several months in 1953 and 1954, what finally happened to the *Manatee* was somewhat of a mystery for many years.

"As we started to hold former shipmate reunions few knew just exactly what happened other than the ship was sold as scrap," Osenton said. "Guesses ranged from being cut up for razor blades to getting itself half-sunk in Baton Rouge. There was even the thought that the ship was saved from the junk heap by giving it in total to Brazil."

So, Osenton did some investigation work and found out from the Navy Department that the ship was sold to Zidell Explorations of Portland, Oregon, December 10, 1973. And, with that information in hand, on his next visit to his home state of Oregon, he did some more sleuthing.

"I visited Zidell's headquarters while I was in Portland," Osenton said. "It's a big outfit, sitting right on the Willamette River, beneath the Ross Island Bridge on the west side of the city. In their lobby they have a beautiful brass and copper steam whistle from the USS *Philippines Sea*. The company has purchased and scrapped more than 300 ships from the Navy, all for the purpose of building barges. Now, they use new steel plates.

"But concerning the *Manatee*, the Portland company not only purchased it, but the *Cacapon* (AO-52) as well, for a combined price of $586,889.99. The *Manatee* arrived in Portland from Long Beach on January 7, 1974, being towed by Pacific Tugboat at a cost of $30,000. Scrapping commenced on February 5, 1974, and was completed on September 5, 1974.

"Company officials told me that they scrapped it for the steel plates, which were then used to build all kinds of barges. They also salvaged and sold all the valves. But I didn't find out about the other stuff, namely electronic equipment, machinery and rigging, but I imagine they went to special marine salvage companies. The *Cacapon* was towed to Tacoma, Washington and scrapped there."

Despite this most unglamorous ending that we now know to be true, it's still hard for many of us former *Manatee* Sailors to accept. A far better ending might be that her metal was melted down and re-shaped into one of those fancy cruisers or aircraft carriers. We might even go along with a few Toyotas... but a barge?

*　　*　　*

As it is with most Sailors stationed on most ships, Sailors who were stationed on the *Manatee* for a period of time often couldn't wait to be either assigned to different duty or discharged completely. Looking back, most of us don't feel that way today. We tend to forget the bad days and remember only the good times. One Sailor, Archie DeRychere, may have said it for all of us. He was stationed on the destroyer USS *Hull* (DD-350) which, along with the *Manatee*, suffered through Hurricane Cobra during World War II. But while the *Manatee* survived, his ship didn't. The *Hull* still lies at the bottom of the ocean, not far from the

146

Philippine Islands. DeRychere was among the seven officers and 55 enlisted men who were rescued out of a crew of 160.

"One can ask, 'How can you love a ship? It's just a piece of steel,'" he said. "But it's not just a piece of steel. It's an accumulation of personalities and people. The captain, the executive officer, all of your shipmates, they all become brothers."

ABOUT THE AUTHOR

**Joe Kraus (left) in life's early paragraphs
and (right) after far too many chapters.**

Joe Kraus spent his high school years in Salem Oregon and was voted most likely to succeed in his North Salem High School journalism class. That was all the encouragement he needed. His first national magazine article was published while he was still in high school. And after his military service and going to college, he ended up as a managing editor on several daily newspapers. Since then some 300 articles has followed, published in more than 60 different national periodicals.

He has founded two national magazines, *Autograph Collector Magazine* and *Child Stars* Magazine, both now are no longer published. This gave more time to focus on his non-fiction books. Joe's first book, *Alive in the Desert*, published in 1978, was used in the popular TV series Air Wolf starring Ernest Borgnine. A revised edition of the book is expected to be released later this year. He also wrote a TV commercial for singer Kris Kristofferson and the script for the 37th Annual Young Artist Awards in Hollywood, California. Out shortly will be his new book, *Desert Rats: They Came With A Pick, A Shovel And A Dream.* He is also co-writing a book with Ron Stovall titled *The Famous & Successful: Their Advice For All Of Us.*

Married to his wife, Karren for nearly 50 years, they have three grown children and six grandchildren.

Illustrations

Original Artwork Credits:
Peter Kraus: **10, 23, 25** (top and bottom)**, 32, 36** (top)**, 44, 47, 53, 63, 69, 85, 90, 94, 97, 109, 118, 132, 137, 140** (bottom)**, 147, 152**

Picture Credits:

Name Index

152

Made in the USA
San Bernardino, CA
18 June 2016